Memoirs of a Child Holocaust Survivor

Memoirs of a Child Holocaust Survivor

Living Without Hatred

A.M. Fox

Pen & Sword
MILITARY

First published in Great Britain in 2025 by
Pen & Sword Military
An imprint of Pen & Sword Books Limited
Yorkshire – Philadelphia

Copyright © A.M. Fox 2025

ISBN 978 1 03611 917 1

The right of A.M. Fox to be identified as
Author of this Work has been asserted by her in accordance
with the Copyright, Designs and Patents Act 1988.

A CIP catalogue record for this book is
available from the British Library.

All rights reserved. No part of this book may be reproduced,
transmitted, downloaded, decompiled or reverse engineered in
any form or by any means, electronic or mechanical including
photocopying, recording or by any information storage and retrieval
system, without permission from the Publisher in writing. No part of
this book may be used or reproduced in any manner for the purpose
of training artificial intelligence technologies or systems.

Typeset by Mac Style
Printed in the UK by CPI Group (UK) Ltd, Croydon, CR0 4YY.

The Publisher's authorised representative in the EU for product
safety is Authorised Rep Compliance Ltd., Ground Floor,
71 Lower Baggot Street, Dublin D02 P593, Ireland.
www.arccompliance.com

For a complete list of Pen & Sword titles please contact

PEN & SWORD BOOKS LIMITED
47 Church Street, Barnsley, South Yorkshire, S70 2AS, England
E-mail: enquiries@pen-and-sword.co.uk
Website: www.pen-and-sword.co.uk
or
PEN AND SWORD BOOKS
1950 Lawrence Road, Havertown, PA 19083, USA
E-mail: uspen-and-sword@casematepublishers.com
Website: www.penandswordbooks.com

To all those who,
whatever they have endured,
choose to retain their humanity.

Contents

Foreword   viii

Fuks and Gotesman family trees   x

Chapter 1   How I Met My Husband   1

Chapter 2   Before the War, Tuszyn, Central Poland, 1930–1939   17

Chapter 3   The War   51

Chapter 4   8 May–14 August 1945   90

Chapter 5   England – a New Life, 14 August 1945–the Present   96

Chapter 6   Epilogue   121

Acknowledgements   124

Foreword

In recent years anti-Jewish hate has, heartbreakingly, been more than a chapter in a history book. Jews across the world have once again experienced a level of antisemitism which was meant to be consigned to books such as this one.

But events since October 7th, have reminded every Jew, and every true anti-racist, quite how fragile civilised society is and how quickly the actions of some can undermine the very fabric of our society and make others feel insecure and unsafe.

These concerns about the current state of our society make this memoir all the more important and all the more timely. In an age of hate, misinformation and populism it should be of no surprise to anyone that many people in my community view current events as the latest chapter in our story of being scapegoated.

As a community, we know where antisemitism can lead. We know what happens when a mob decides to target and blame one community for the world's ills. We know what can happen when politicians choose to embrace hate rather than protect their citizens.

Which is why this memoir of Chaim, of Harry, is both timely and a must read. When some try to rewrite our history, to distort facts and dismiss the fear of those being marginalised, personal stories become all the more important.

6 million Jews dead, one and half million Jewish children murdered, hundreds of thousands of disabled, LGBT+, and Roma massacred and

millions of political prisoners and others killed. These numbers are too big for us to comprehend, too many for us to really appreciate the real scale of what happened. It is only by understanding and bearing witness to the individual stories of the victims that we can appreciate the full horror and be reminded of what can happen when good people do nothing.

It is in this tradition that A. M. Fox has written this memoir and we should be forever grateful to her for sharing Harry's story and for writing so beautifully about such horrors.

May his memory and all those touched by the Shoah be a blessing.

Baroness Anderson of Stoke-on-Trent

The Fuks family tree

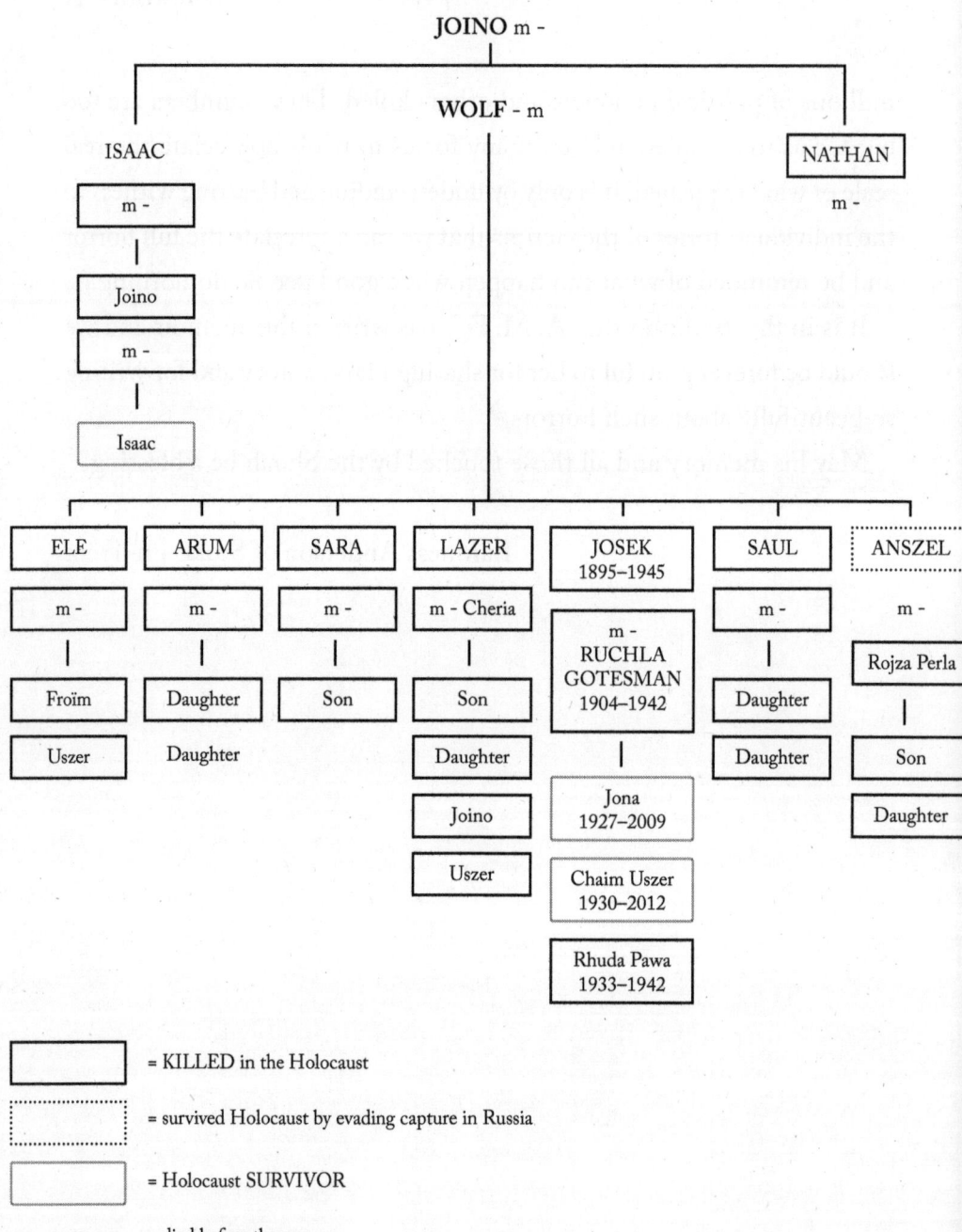

The Gotesman family tree

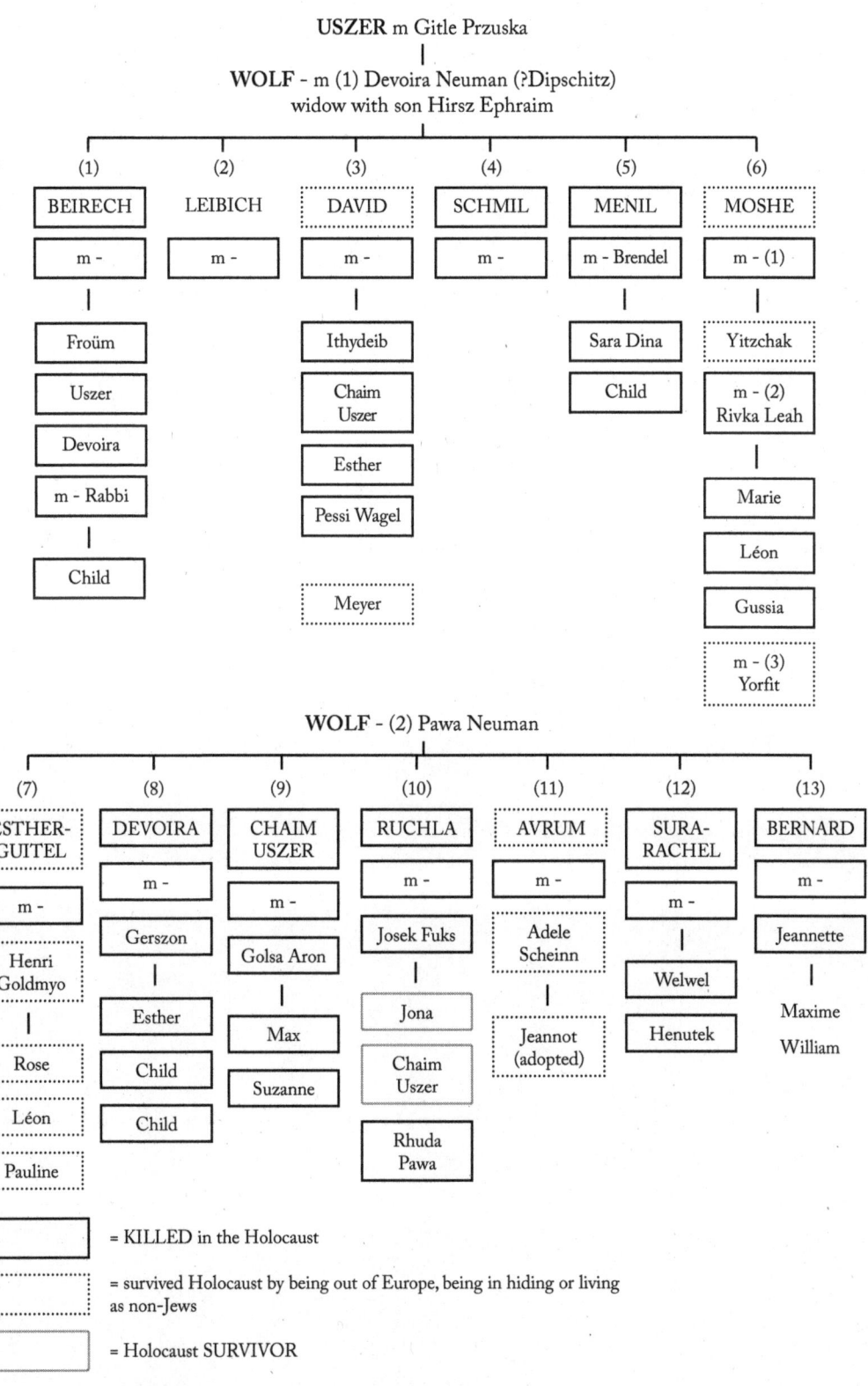

Chapter 1

How I Met My Husband

I had never wanted to feature in my husband's story, but he insisted. Martin Gilbert insisted also, hence the opening chapter.

At the age of twelve I was tall and lanky. Called a beanpole by one of my teachers, this awkward state masked a heart beating with romantic longings which were constantly being stoked by a passion for music, literature and all the arts. The cinema idols of the time provided hours of dreaming, too. My friends and I indulged in these fantasies under our scratchy school blankets, whispering into the darkness of the dorm our shared visions of lives filled with endless bliss, noble endeavour and breathless excitement. A group of us sniffled for days after a showing of *A Tale of Two Cities*; our misery remaining intact in spite of the celluloid breaking in two more than once during the film's projection. Emotions were close to the surface, and we were positively overcome with grief as Dirk Bogarde, with whom we were all in love, ascended the steps of Madame La Guillotine and did his 'far, far better thing'. Mr Rochester, Mr Darcy and many other literary heroes were all romantic attachments of the highest order for me, and I read and re-read such books, feeling that they contained the secret meaning of life itself (which is LOVE, so of course, they do!)

I was being educated at a boarding school which was owned and run by an Anglican Convent, although about half the teachers and auxiliary staff were not nuns. The school was situated in a small market town several miles away from its very rural prep school where I had been since the age of ten. Now twelve, this was my first term in the upper school. The compulsory thick blue stockings pulled down uncomfortably on my suspender belt, and my total naïvety in matters of the world was exposed. The two most important revelations of that autumn term of 1963 both came via the same senior girl. I remember her face, and her name, and I will be grateful to her always. The first eye-opener came during Confirmation classes, which were given to small groups by the house sister, a nun. We were dealing with the Ten Commandments and came to number seven, *Thou shalt not commit adultery*. Always keen to elicit 'difficult' information from the nuns, this taboo was lingered over with as much attention to detail as we could muster. We 'knew little' but delighted in making the poor sister concerned turn pink. In our group we were all the same age, except for the senior girl mentioned who had somehow missed out on Confirmation earlier.

She questioned sweetly, 'Do you mean like Christine Keeler, Sister?'

The Profumo/Keeler scandal was going on at the time, and the reference caused some hesitation on the part of the nun.

I asked, 'Who is Christine Keeler? What did she do?'

I had no idea but sensed a bit of spice. After all, our biblical favourites were the juicy bits in Leviticus, and despite the fact that we were mostly ignoramuses we possessed a keen thirst to improve our knowledge in this field.

The nun's dubiety went on a bit, causing the older girl to say kindly, 'Would you like *me* to explain to her, Sister?'

'Oh, yes please,' came the relieved reply. 'Perhaps you *could* talk to her later?'

Thus it was that I was introduced to the facts of life in graphic detail, and at the same time told what it meant to be a prostitute, and what it meant to have an affair. The works in fact, and I was both intrigued and rather horrified, as my knowledge until this point had consisted of the contents of a small blue booklet left on my bed at home, a few days before going to prep school … and containing a rather sketchy explanation of menstruation. There was NO conversation at home in those days about such matters.

The second revelation came through a book. At the bottom of the school's sweeping staircase there were some large bookcases, whose dark polished shelves contained novels and other tomes deemed to be recreational and uplifting. We were allowed to take these books out whenever we wanted to, and as an avid reader I was there often. Whilst nosing about on one occasion, a copy of Anne Franks's *Diary* was suddenly put into my hand by the senior girl of Confirmation class fame.

'This is very good,' she told me.

With her recent credentials in enlightenment giving her considerable status, I trusted her judgement totally and took the book with anticipation. I remember beginning to read it. I was open to it but unprepared for what it would do to me. I could feel the claustrophobia of Anne's hiding place and I was also able to identify with some of her adolescent emotions as I was roughly the same age, but when I came upon the family's betrayal and the footnotes as to what followed I remember the shock and the sadness. Something that had been terrible, but rather vague, to do with Jews and the war, now descended upon my very soul with stark reality.

That autumn, Anne Frank's *Diary* sat as an uncomfortable weight on my chest and changed everything. It was not as if any of us was unaware or unaffected by the war; all our parents had been involved in it in some capacity. Nor were we were a generation treated with kid gloves, for we were children that had been brought up to have an essentially robust attitude to hardship. Anne Frank's fate sickened me because it was so inglorious and unnecessary. She and her family were not spies or the enemy in uniform, nor had they been innocent victims of bombing or heroes of the Resistance. Hunted, hidden, afraid, betrayed and then killed simply for their race and religion, there was no excuse for their destruction. Anne had cut film stars out of magazines and dreamed of them, just as we did. Her heart was longing for romance just as ours were. I learnt about evil in that term, the scale of which was beyond belief, and still is.

Some of our school customs probably dated back to pre-1914! We changed into afternoon dresses for tea and prep and were expected to behave like young ladies of the 'nicer' variety, with good manners and the anticipation of marriage. Academic rigour came a rather poor second in the ethos of the establishment, but there was a certain open mindedness to the vagaries of growing girls and much understanding of our questing intellects, if not their training, which does great credit to the nuns, most of whom were Oxbridge graduates. They turned not a hair as in our childish political ignorance Mao's Little Red Book was passed around, for example, but I did not feel able to talk about Anne Frank's *Diary*. How could I explain that I no longer felt twelve but a hundred and twelve, swamped by outrage at the injustice I had just become aware of, and aching to put some love into the abyss that now seemed to exist in the world after all that hatred and murder.

* * *

Brown envelopes stuffed with ancient photographs were kept in the bottom drawer of my mother's bureau. Some of the family photos reached back into the mid-nineteenth century, when photography began, and these precious and very beautiful images linked me with and rooted me with the past, helping to give me a sense of where I came from and who

I was. When I was a child and stayed with my grandmother, I asked her on each visit if she might let me look again in the Victorian red leather box which contained some cardboard-mounted portraits. How I enjoyed gazing at them! It never bored me, and I loved asking questions about the people concerned, especially as one of my great-grandmothers had been full of 'delicious' eccentricities of character. This indomitable lady possessed qualities of reforming zeal, artistic talent and compassion, as well as her fearless and entertaining quirkiness, and the tales about her were ones I loved to hear again and again. One escapade came about due to a spate of fruit thefts from the orchard. The fruit would have been given away, I was told, but she took a dim view of it being pilfered. A solution was sought, and night after night for a week she dressed up in a sheet and, with a dim lantern held underneath it, she paraded through the fruit trees at midnight. After this, no fruit was ever stolen again! A great-great-grandmama (the mother of this creative fruit tree lady) used to pass her glass over the finger bowl at the main meal, 'for the King over the water', I was informed. Our family had been staunch Jacobites, and the rather stern visage of this grand old lady was examined with great intensity, and questions asked.

Now that the red box is with me, the pleasure of looking through its treasures is undimmed, but these old photos do more than give delight. I made use of them, for example, when my dearly loved father was ill. Sometimes I was up in the night waiting for nurses to come 'in an hour's time' at 2.00 or 3.00 am, and in a bid to stay awake I would open a brown envelope or two and look at the bygone faces of my family. Not only did this stave off sleep it gave me a certain courage and tranquillity. Century and more past fashions may appear all frills and furbelows, but these clothes belonged to people who had borne responsibility with true feeling and had demonstrably not shirked from the calling we all have as humans, to be of service to others. They had left examples of unselfishness and sometimes bravery which were inspiring to me in the chilly wee small hours. I was so glad that I had asked about the people depicted and had listened to family stories from my grandmother and others, and I hoped that they all knew *somehow* in heaven that they were still being of use.

* * *

Asked the question, 'If your house was on fire what possession would you grab as you fled the building?' so many people say that they would take a particular photograph, and after such events it is often the loss of these irreplaceable images that hurts the most. Pictures are not life itself, but following any disaster when home and family are destroyed it becomes an additional hurt and sadness not to have photographs and be able to look at the faces of those to whom one has belonged.

As a Holocaust Survivor, my husband was very fortunate in having been given a few photographs. These rare prints had been in the possession of relatives in France, who had moved there from Poland in the 1920s and who had survived the Nazis by living as non-Jews or going into hiding. A few years ago, when he was visiting relations in Paris, a cousin held up an old photo.

'Does anyone know who this person is standing at the back?'

An uncle who would have known was no longer alive, and now there seemed to be nobody left who could recognize the woman standing behind the seated family group. My husband took the picture and his heart missed a beat.

'That's my mother!' he said. 'That's my mother!'

It was a great feeling for him, almost overwhelming for a time. He had been given one photo of her some years before (Plate 8), but this new and different likeness was a most wonderful and unexpected discovery. It must have been taken, my husband thinks, in 1924, as a farewell photo, just before that aunt and her family emigrated to France. Harry's mother joined them for the photograph, almost certainly before she was married later in that year (Plate 10: and Plate 11 the same family established in France). Many of our friends are survivors who came through the war and found at the end of it that they were quite alone, with no family left alive and no photographs to sustain them and link them to all those who mean so much.

One of the photographs saved in France is quite small and faded; it depicts two small boys holding hands. The elder boy clutches a ball and smiles at the camera, whilst the younger one is holding a stick and has a small hoop hanging over his arm. He's a sturdy wee fellow and looks at the camera with a somewhat enigmatic expression, uncertain perhaps that photography is worth his game being interrupted. I search their faces for clues as to how they were then, for the date of the picture is the early 1930s, and the place is Central Poland, where the brothers are playing on their family's land in the Forest of Tuszyn. The elder boy would become my brother-in-law. The younger one became my husband (Plate 1).

* * *

In the spring of 1983, fifty years after that photograph was taken, I accepted a request to act as a steward in the church of St George's in the East, which was hosting an exhibition from Auschwitz. I was then an Anglican nun in London's East End, where the Jewish and Christian communities of all denominations had come together wanting to reveal and combat the curse of racism, especially in the light of increased National Front activity. This exhibition showed the ultimate consequences of racial hatred, and I remember that it had Kalashnikov-armed guards at the entrance. Auschwitz had lent examples of all it had, and there were train tickets, suitcases, photographs, shoes, piles of human hair and many other items from its tragic collection, with everything most carefully labelled and explained. The historian in Auschwitz was a Dr Franciszek Piper, who had come over with the precious items, and we had many long talks together. He was passionate in his efforts to ensure that the terrible truth of the Holocaust should be exposed as fully as possible, with its heinous historical significance widely laid bare, in the bid for there to be tolerance between peoples, and respect for human life.

Two films were on continuous showing in St George's, one being the well-known footage of the Russian liberation of Auschwitz, the other telling a story that still haunts me. Its soundtrack was a tinny version of Chopin's Funeral March, played over and over again against the silence of the otherwise silent film. A group of primary-aged school children with their teacher stand together in what seems to be a disused airfield. The young boys and girls are gathered close to each other in a ragged line and are simply staring ahead. Two or three SS guards with their dogs are standing with the children, and the guards appear relaxed. One of the boys has a toy catapult and he suddenly flicks something from it. At once the schoolmaster places a restraining hand on his arm, but he need not have worried; a guard waves his hand, indicating that all is well and he is only too pleased to allow his dog to 'go fetch'. A Red Cross-marked lorry arrives and the group clambers in. Only the teacher understands what this means and what will happen, and as the guards close the truck he looks intently up at the sky. Carefully, calmly and without any hurry or emotion, one of the guards fits a thick hose over the exhaust pipe, then fastens the other end of the hose onto a fitting that leads directly into the sealed truck. He does this as if he were doing a mundane job of work in a garage. Once the hose is screwed into place he signals casually to the driver that all is ready. The truck then drives off. The tinny Chopin continues to play for a while, and then the film ends. What was this little scene of murder where children and their teacher could be alive and well one minute and choking to death the next? Where was the war? The children had no guns. The teacher had no guns.

After each session in the exhibition, I would bicycle back to the convent in a state of frozen horror. I needed the journey home as a transition into contemporary life, as it felt almost impossible to 'slot back in' straight away. I felt that if I was asked to 'pass the mustard', I would say, 'What *is* mustard?' Each human life is without price, and how we all loved and respected those around us in the East End. To be exposed to such wholesale murder in the exhibition was a considerable challenge, but one I felt I had to rise to. After all, whatever feelings I had, they were NOTHING compared to the real-life anguish, and to say 'yes' to the request to be a steward seemed the very least that I could do.

All the guides at this exhibition were Holocaust Survivors, and I discovered years later that it had made some of them ill. It was the first time that they had been called upon to witness to their suffering in public, and the exhibits were harrowing indeed. One of the survivors began to talk to me. Words poured out of him. Over many days, and during all the weeks of the exhibition, he sought me out, and we sat down on the edge of a platform while he told me more and more. He said that he had never talked like this before. It was he who told me that he was part of a group of child Holocaust Survivors, who had been invited by King George VI to come over to England together not long after the war ended, and that they had since formed a charity in the 1960s in order to help others. They called their charity the '45 Aid Society, after the year of their liberation. They were also known as 'The Boys'. My husband-to-be was amongst a group from 'The Boys' asked to help as guides. He did it once. This was before any of them had given talks about their experiences, and he found it impossible to keep explaining to visitors over and over again what the piles of human hair meant, what all the items were, what the gas chambers meant. He had been surprised to see nuns there and must have seen me, but although he came to the meal marking the end of the exhibition, we never met.

Some time before the Auschwitz exhibition was held, I was working in a Hoxton parish. A recent photograph was shown me of one of the National Front's founders. He was upright and wearing a pseudo-Nazi uniform. Beside him on the ground was a large yellow can. The label on this can was in clear print and stated, 'This weed killer can kill x thousand Jews'. This was the late1970s, not the 1940s!

* * *

For several years when in the convent I was greatly privileged to be one of the chaplains for St Joseph's Hospice in Hackney. A lot of living had gone on since I stumbled across Anne Frank when I was twelve, and the question of the Holocaust had been put into a deep place inside me. One day in the hospice I became aware that an old lady was looking at me intently.

I went over to her, and whilst holding out her hand to me, before she said anything else she said, 'I'm Jewish, but it doesn't matter – does it?'

I took her hand and sat down. 'OF COURSE NOT!' I wanted to reply, but she beat me to it saying, 'I'm Jewish, but it's the same God – isn't it?'

What I said I have no idea now, but we became great friends. She had walked with her baby half across Europe to escape the Nazis, managing somehow to get a boat to England and ending up in London. With no English and a baby to feed, she got herself a job in Lyons' Corner House. The manager saw how efficient she was and after a month or two asked if she knew how to order and manage the stores. Saying yes, but with no notion of what to do, she took over this job, and necessity won the day. By the end of her working life she had been promoted to the top echelons of the company. I must have known this amazing lady before the Auschwitz exhibition and her initial words jolted me. It shocked me that she betrayed her underlying wounds in that way, wounds that had never healed in all the intervening years, and I realized that the Holocaust was certainly not over.

* * *

As the decade moved from the 1980s to the 1990s I was released from religious life. Shortly after returning to the world, I was received into the Roman Catholic Church in the Crypt of Westminster Cathedral, with just a few friends around me during a private Mass, celebrated by a friend who was a priest in the Cathedral. Becoming a Catholic was not due to 'rejection' of the Episcopal/Anglican church. It was rather a 'coming home'. At the age of nine I had purchased a second-hand book for sixpence called *The Pope Laughs*. This detailed some amusing vignettes from the life of Pope John XXIII. At the end of the book was an invitation to request a correspondence course about becoming a Catholic. I sent off for it and recall the plain buff envelopes with their typed sheets arriving each week. Boarding school came when I was ten, however, and eventually religious life. The Community I joined was 'more Catholic than the Catholics'. We used the RC rite at Mass and the full breviary. This was permitted as we had a private chapel; the priests who served us were of the High Church persuasion and never seemed to mind. My journey to becoming a Catholic is not for this story, except to say that when I met Harry I was a Catholic, and he knew this. He insisted on driving me to Mass, in fact, and came with me three times a year, at Christmas, Easter and Mothering Sunday. Later, our daughter did this also, and I always went to *Shul* (Yiddish for school/synagogue) with them. Harry talked about 'being made all right' about churches because of this. As a child, due to antisemitism, he was taught to walk on the opposite side of the road if he saw a church – to keep safe! (A sad indictment indeed on the Catholic Church of that time in Poland.) He was surprised to discover Christians used the Psalms, and how much of all the Hebrew Scriptures came into the readings. He told me more than once that he envied my faith. He *wanted* to believe in God, but after all that had happened in his life, he 'couldn't' – he just hoped that I was RIGHT!

Once, when our daughter was very small and we were all three in church, she suddenly called out in a loud voice as the priest came in, 'Here comes the Rabbi!' (*Shul* was usually once a week, and her spirit of fraternity between faiths delighted me – and would have pleased Pope Francis, I think!)

* * *

On 3 August 1991 at three o'clock in the afternoon I knocked at the door of a fourth-floor flat in London, but there was no answer. In the end I sat down on the carpet outside and waited. It had been about eighteen months since I had been released from my religious state and had 'returned to the world'. This had not been due to any loss of faith, as indicated; rather it had come to me as a further call into life. Now, less than two months after turning forty, I was doing some research and I remembered that group of Holocaust Survivors known as 'The Boys'.

Older survivors had written their stories, and their post-war lives were known about, but this group had been so young, and their suffering came at such a vulnerable point in their growing up, it seemed important to discover more.

This visit was in order to meet the last one of them that I had arranged to interview. At first I had attempted to find the 'Boy' who had talked to me so much at the Auschwitz exhibition, only to discover that he had sadly died; but I was most kindly given other contacts, and each one had been generous with their time and with their stories. Now, as time went past sitting on the carpet, I became uncertain about what to do; but having made this arrangement, I decided to continue to wait. Eventually, the lift doors opened and Harry Fox stepped out carrying a bulging briefcase.

'Ah!' says he. 'I am sorry to be late.'

We go in.

'Tea, coffee?' he calls.

'Coffee, please,' say I.

'Milk, sugar?'

'Just milk please.'

A grinning face appears from behind a cupboard door.

'Ah! You're cheap to run!'

His smile was infectious, his energy boundless and his charm totally irresistible. Harry was twenty years older than I, but he seemed far, far younger. He was physically very fit, and his whole demeanour was lively and youthful.

The questions I was asking him were about the war and, fearing that they would cause pain, I was being as careful and sensitive as possible. Harry was a talker and did not hesitate to answer me, but he was able to digress as well, and we never seemed to finish! We went on to have several encounters over the next weeks, and then to my astonishment,

I found myself singing in the street one day. I had now been out of the convent for almost twenty-one months, but I felt sixteen again and realized that I had fallen in love! Harry was a Polish Jew. He had been married before, but at the time we met he had been divorced for several years; of his three children, two were in their early twenties and one in their teens. From our first meeting he made me smile inside, and I fell hook, line and sinker for this man who had such a zest for life after all he had endured. This did not mean that the path of love ran smoothly, for I pushed away his initial advances, feeling that we were both very vulnerable. I often worked late and would rush home just before 10.00 pm to make sure I was there when he rang. I remember playing the same CD of French café songs, night after night, as I waited for his 'phone call. It was wonderful to find that he had feelings for me, and we weathered all the romantic shemozzles. He proposed to me seventeen months after we first met. We got married five weeks later by Special Licence. Not a long engagement! Two and a half years later we were blessed with a child.

Harry had taken to the tradition of reading the paper over breakfast, and one morning he was reading a *Times* obituary. Suddenly he let out a great guffaw. A Jewish comedian had died, and the paper carried some of his jokes. Anyone observing this incident would have seen a healthy-looking man whose face was alight with laughter. He looked as if his life had been one of security and contentment, but I am aware that he continually *chooses life*, through thick and thin, as Moses bade the earlier Israelites do. He dives into this life head first, bravely and optimistically. It can knock him sideways, and I have witnessed some severely distressing knocks since knowing him, but he comes up again ready to go forward, seizing the moment and using the day. He and the other 'Boys' I know have emerged from the brink of annihilation and know how precious life is.

One very dear friend amongst 'The Boys', Kopel Kendall, held me riveted in awe and astonishment some years ago when he began rolling about on the floor, tears of laughter streaming down his face, as he told me of the time when he woke up in a cattle truck to find somebody had 'shit on his face' whilst he was asleep, making his face 'all yellow'. Jokes about the situations of the war and the Camps are essential, and I realized this, but to listen to the camaraderie and lack of self-pity between the 'Boys' is a lesson in human dignity and a wonder to behold. Even now, after over twenty years of knowing them, I may need a tissue, but usually because of laughter, and I have sometimes wanted ear plugs, as they never hesitate to talk all at once and will raise their voices to enable them to carry on a conversation over the heads of several others, should the need arise. They are, however, a testament in this cynical age to the real victory of the human spirit, their victory over monumental human degradation and cruelty.

* * *

This book is something of Harry's story and includes all he is able to recall of that vanished world of his childhood, its people and their way of life. Memories from before the Nazis are especially important to him and are also his greatest attempt at providing a memorial to all who were killed so savagely. They are a 'shout' which says that he and his family *lived*, and they lived in a manner to be proud of. They considered each other, and in the Jewish community where he was brought up, they all looked after each other. Life was hard, but the values and lessons of childhood still inform and guide him. Harry's memories of the war, however, unlike the memories of older Holocaust Survivors, contain little of his emotions. 'It was all terrible' is the most I have been able to elicit from him, but this is very honest. He has had to put an emotional lid on this time to a considerable extent in order to be able to live, and he refuses to embroider anything now. In some of the incidents described, though, there *are* hints to be had of his character, and pointers to his unconquerable spirit do reveal themselves. It is the story of a boy who became a man almost overnight, and there are episodes which testify to his astonishing and selfless courage, not to mention his natural cheek, which even in the dire circumstances of Nazi terror held him in good stead. The story does not end with the war, either, and as a chronicle it reveals a fascinating glimpse of how a child, who had turned nine less than two months before the war began and who was still less than fifteen when it ended, emerged from the Holocaust, not unscathed, but undefeated.

Chapter 2

Before the War, Tuszyn, Central Poland, 1930–1939

A note concerning names

(Pronunciation, spelling and general usage)

It is common for the same person to be referred to or called by several variations of their name, often within one sentence! The spelling of people's names has proved to be extremely varied, and translating words in general from Yiddish is imprecise, using phonetics.

'Ch' is pronounced as in the Scottish word loch.

Chaim = Life

Devoira = Deborah

'J' is pronounced as 'Y', hence Josek/Jossel being spoken as 'Yosek/Yossel'. As Harry's father Josek was always known as Jossel, this is how I have referred to him in the text. Josek = Joseph

'W' is pronounced as 'V,' so Volf, Velvo, Velvol, Pava, etc.

Hebrew/Yiddish names have many different spellings and adaptations in other languages. For example, Esther-Gitle becomes Esther-Guitel in France. Guitel is pronounced 'Geetel'. Yitzchak became 'Jacques' in Belgium and France, but Harry and I always called him Yitzchak, using the Yiddish, as this was how Harry had known of him since childhood.

This is Harry's story, and I have used Harry rather than Chaim Uszer in the text, as that was how he was known predominantly since coming to England.

As these are Holocaust memoirs I have used Jona for Harry's elder brother, as that was how Harry referred to him when talking about Poland and the war, and how Jona referred to himself, certainly at that time. Jona (Joino) became John Fox, or Johnny, after coming to the UK. Harry and some others of the 'Boys' also called him Jona or Joino as well as John or Johnny.

Ruchla was always called 'Ruchel' in the family, so this diminutive is used in the text.

Ruchla = Rachel/Rachael and pronounced 'Roo'ch'la/Roo'ch'el'.

Soup = the disgusting evil smelling water with a few pieces of kohlrabi (a variety of German cabbage) or some flakes of potato floating in it was always referred to as 'a' soup. 'A' soup was universal language in all the Camps.

'Sz' as in Anszel and Uszer is pronounced 'sh': hence Harry writing it in English as Chaim Usher. Harry said his immediate family never used the hyphen for him. Uncle Chaim-Uszer and others of that name in the family did seem to use it.

Harry's childhood was tough but very good. He knew he was loved at home, and he fitted into the homes of his numerous extended family with pleasure and gusto. There were so many colourful characters to come across and quite literally 'never a dull moment'. His naturally eager nature often got him into trouble, but he also revelled in the diversity he encountered and he took it all in. He is a person who always 'takes on' a situation rather than somebody content to be an observer. The Jewish way of life in Poland during the 1930s, the life that he knew as a boy, was wiped out, but never expunged from his mind and heart.

Harry remembers his home vividly, and everything in that special house on Remishfesvkego Street, Tuszyn is clear to him. He is able to shut his eyes and roam through the rooms, allowing himself to pause here and there in order to recapture a childhood scene. There is his father standing over the big cutting table working on a coat; or he can look again at the glowing painted floral decorations that his mother had stencilled onto the walls to brighten things up. His earliest memory, though, dates from the family's first house and is still quite distinct and intense. He is three, the age of the boy in the photograph (Plate 1) and he is at home asking for his mother. No, he is told, he cannot see her at the moment she is busy. He makes a rumpus. His mother would never be too busy to see him, there must be a mistake! He heads for the closed door but is held back. Protesting loudly, with his chin no doubt sticking out, he is reduced to tears, but Jossel, his father, is unrelenting. Later, the cause of his misery is revealed as being the birth of his little sister, Rhuda-Pawa.

Rhuda-Pawa was born in the house where Harry and his elder brother were also born. This house was small, having just two rooms. Houses of one or two rooms for an entire family were commonplace.

Ruchla, known usually as Ruchel, their mother, wanted a better life than this for her family, especially as there were now five of them, and she said to her husband, 'It might be all right for your brothers to live in one room, but we want a house.'

She had a fine intelligence and craved for more than an existence of simply 'making do', and it was under her impetus that Jossel took possession of the bigger four-roomed house next door. This house had been a *Gemina*, an administration place for the Jewish Council, and it is this house that would be home from when Harry was four until the end of November 1939. Jossel had bought well, and most of the large yard became his upon the purchase of the new house. This meant that they were now the owners of a garden, as well as a stable for their horse. There was even space to spare, and Jossel would utilize this in the future, building another house there as a further means of supporting his family (Plate 5).

Remishfesvkego Street was punctuated with shops, and near to their home there was a shoemaker's, a grocer's and a shop that made and sold pots and pans. Opposite, on the other side of the road, there was a solicitor's, not to mention aunts, uncles and cousins, both in the same street and at every turn. As with a lot of the private houses in Tuszyn, theirs did not have a front door that opened onto the street. A passage off the road had a door on each side of it leading on into the yard beyond. The door on the left of their passage was that of their first small house; the door on the right belonged to their new bigger home. Once you came through the right-hand door you were immediately in the main room of the house. This room had many functions, being the family's kitchen, dining room, work room and general living space. What a lovely room it was! On opening the passage door, you were in a place which was big and full of the light which came pouring in from several large windows that looked out into Remishfesvkego Street to the right. Standing in the middle of it all was Jossel's cutting table. This table was at least twelve feet in length, and its top was several inches thick. It seemed to communicate its ongoing usefulness and its capacity to assist in hard work of the kind that would endure, passing down the generations so that father and son and son's sons would still stand there bent over their cloth. This table, barely altered with age, was 'always there', solid, strong and comforting, silently holding the memories of the family. Sixty years later, Harry can still touch its thick wood in his mind's eye and linger over it. On special days – and a special day happened once a week – the table became endowed with other qualities. It would be cleared of all work and covered with a white cloth. Extra nice food would be laid upon it, and the atmosphere changed from commerce to religion. This was a time for meetings of family and friends, when they would eat, talk and pray together as their ancestors had done for several thousand years before on the Sabbath. There were two tailoring sewing machines, treadle machines, in this room. These were placed against the back wall and would be covered with white cloths, not every week but just on important celebrations, adding to the mystery and difference of those occasions.

Every day, the room buzzed with life and energy. Work and purpose breathed in and out, and this place was the hub and centre of Harry's home. A smaller table served the family for weekday meals, which were cooked on a black kitchen range with four rings that stood on the left of the front doorway. Harry's mother was also able to cook on parts of the top which had no rings, but which were nevertheless hot. The range was fuelled by coal, but in the middle of winter when it was very cold a separate special oven which was run on sawdust kept them warm. This oven fed pipes that ran all around the room.

In addition to this main room there were two bedrooms and a storeroom. It was a good house, not a hovel, and Harry still feels that glow of pleasure remembering it and finding it had been a place from where he could go out and hold his head high.

The first bedroom led directly off the main room and belonged to Harry and his brother Jona. They had a bed each, and there was a table there as well, with an oven in the wall which provided heat for this room as well as the bedroom beyond, where Harry's mother, father and little sister slept. In order to be able to get into their room, these three had to pass through the boys' room, but this was never a problem or an issue of any kind. Many families they knew had to manage with only one bedroom between them all, with frequently more than one to a bed. Harry's family arrangements were something of a luxury.

The fourth room at home was the smallest and the one Jossel used for storing things. On Tuesdays, however, it was rented out to some people who came in from the town of Belchatow (Wolbish in Yiddish) and became a shop for selling wool. Jossel never used the room himself as a place from which to sell his own goods, but he let it out on Tuesdays as that was the Tuszyn market day, and still is.

Tuszyn lies in the middle of Poland and was a small and inconspicuous locale when Harry lived there (Plate 2). Set in the middle of the countryside, it was not totally isolated, however, being only about twelve miles from the far larger industrial town of Łódź. Tuszyn had been the home of at least ten generations of the family on Jossel's side, and when Harry was growing up, his paternal extended family were very numerous. There were at least eighty Fuks-connected relatives in Tuszyn, for Great-Grandfather Joino Fuks had many siblings, not shown on the family tree, who had also had descendants. There were several maternal relatives as well, which meant that there were approximately a hundred relations to be found within walking distance!

Tuszyn was certainly not a metropolis in the 1930s; rather, it was a 'one horse' sort of place, where the inhabitants would joke that if a horse were to stand in the town centre, its head would stick out at one end with its tail protruding from the other. It had a population of approximately a thousand Jews and a thousand Poles, which worked out at about two hundred and fifty households apiece. Tuszyn may not have been a substantial town but it made up for this by being a bustling place, especially when its busy and thriving market much more than doubled the population once a week.

Farmers came to the market from far and wide, to sell their own produce, but especially to buy clothes and other necessary goods. In size Tuszyn was no more than a village and had only been elevated to the status of a town at all as a reward. The ancient story tells of a young Polish prince who had got himself completely lost. His grieving parents scoured the land for him and, after much searching, their tender-aged offspring was found alive and well in Tuszyn, whereupon his happy family promoted the place out of gratitude!

Harry's family lived alongside the other Jewish families in the central part of the town, while the non-Jews, who were Catholics and tended to be farmers, lived around the periphery. This situation had probably evolved during the years when Jews were not permitted to own land and were therefore not able to be farmers. The two peoples traded together, often went to school together and frequently liked the same kind of food. The Jewish families, however, did experience antisemitism and lived under a cloud of scarcely veiled hostility. Harry and his brother were taught from early on that, amongst other things, it was not safe to leave their area after dark for fear of being attacked. If they did need to go out of the Jewish area they would take their big guard dog with them for protection.

The Sabbath is kept by Jews from sundown on Friday until sundown on Saturday, but when the Catholic community were walking to church on Sunday and saw Jews at work, some of them would react with indignation, throwing stones that broke workshop windows. Insults were shouted: 'Bloody Jew, works on Sunday!' They forgot that a holy day had been observed, but on the day before. This situation was aggravated by the fact that the main church of Tuszyn was in the Jewish part of the town. When stones and insults were hurled at Jossel, there came a time when he had had enough of it. For once indignation got the better of *him*, and he came out and hit the perpetrator with a charcoal-filled iron. This man took Jossel to court, but in a small town the judge knew everyone and knew their characters.

'I'll make a deal with you,' said the judge to the Pole. 'If you stop abusing *him*, I can guarantee that he will no longer hit *you*.'

Harry learned quickly how to take care of himself. Fists were often required, and he discovered that he was physically very strong. Uncomfortable as their situation was, it was lived with and put up with as part and parcel of the everyday, and the everyday was in other respects full and vibrant, especially for children. Apart from immediate family there were so many cousins to play with and so many uncles and aunts to visit! Being a member of an old established family that had lived in the same place for several hundred years gave a measure of confidence to a child growing up, and the family was a respected one, looked up to by Jews and Christians alike. Gazing back on it all now, Harry recalls that there was so much LIFE going on, and so many people with whom he had connections and relationships.

Everyone that Harry knew worked very hard, for Poland in the 1930s was a place that demanded hard work, and making a living was a continuous struggle. For adults, it was indeed a diet of work, work, work, with only the rhythm of religion breaking up the week. Any recreation was undertaken seriously when it could be had. Children worked hard also, but they knew how to play. They had no cinema, but in addition to their own games, a travelling Yiddish theatre would come to Tuszyn from time to time, and Harry remembers a song about a man who wanted to kill his wife! Passing groups of jugglers, singers and musicians came through, as well as the occasional sports entertainments – a pole-vaulting spectacle stands out. Plenty of beggars came through, too, and they would knock at the door asking for money.

Jossel would say, 'Are you hungry?' and give them a loaf of bread instead.

Harry's childhood contained some hardships by today's standards, but it was a time full of richness and meaning in which the struggles of life drew people together.

Josek Fuks (Plate 4), always known as Jossel, Harry's father, was born in Tuszyn in 1895 and was the fifth of seven children, six boys and one girl. Jossel's father, Grandfather Wolf Fuks, had died before Harry was born. He had been a tailor, as were his father and grandfather, going back through the generations. Grandfather's children all worked at home with him in the tailoring trade until they left to get married and set up in business on their own. Ele was the eldest, and Harry remembers seeing Ele with his own two sons working with him. After Ele then followed Avrum and Lazer, with Jossel coming in between Aunt Sara and Uncle Saul. Anszel was the youngest, born in 1900 (see Fuks family tree. Fuks is the Polish spelling of the German surname Fuchs, meaning Fox).

Slim and wiry, a 'tough guy' of about five feet nine inches in height, Jossel was clean shaven and well dressed in the latest modern way. Harry thinks he was in fact 'quite a dresser' and he remembers his father in winter sporting a long coat with a Persian lamb collar which he had made for himself. This coat cut such a dash that Jossel was always having to part with it, selling it almost off his back as people came up to him and wanted a 'coat, just like yours'. Jossel would then make himself another coat, only for the story to be repeated! Fashion was one thing, but in observance to Jewish tradition he always wore a round hat when outside, similar to those worn by Jona and Harry in the photograph of them as small children (Plate 1). When at home in the house he was bareheaded, except for mealtimes, when he would always cover his head. Deeply serious and observant about his religion, he was not a zealot, as the absence of a beard in those days shows. Jossel was intelligent and amongst his siblings was known as 'the brains of the family'. He was a man of vigour in every way and enjoyed walking very much. It was quite well known that Jossel was a speedy walker; in fact, he walked so quickly that people used to tell him not to go so fast.

'*Geinisasoyschnell!*' they would shout in Yiddish from across the street. 'Slow down!'

Harry remembers walking with him, especially in the holiday resort of Tuszyn Las, the Forest of Tuszyn, and it being a struggle to keep up. Jossel would talk to his youngest son on these walks, pointing out to him with great pride in his voice that this was their own land, for Jossel was pleased to be a man of property.

Harry noticed his father and took in his every detail from a respectful distance. Jossel worked very hard physically, but this was nothing in comparison to his mind, which was always active. Each week on Friday, he went into Łódź by tram in order to purchase cloth, choosing to do this job on Friday mornings, since because of the Sabbath there was only half a day for work in any case. Harry accompanied him once and was thrilled to have been asked to go with his father. This trip was the only time that Harry ever went into Łódź before the war.

Jossel designed and made all kinds of ready-to-wear coats and trousers. One popular line was long or short cloth overcoats. These were known as car coats, without there being any cars (!), or at least very few. For winter use he made heavy cloth coats that were lined with fur on the inside for warmth. When things were very busy he would work all day and half the night, in spite of having employed a man to assist him with the machining work. (This man's name was Joino, like Harry's brother.) Jossel was good at his job and known for his high quality workmanship. Market day was especially advantageous for business with the Polish farmers who had come into town, and most of his garments were sold to them. Jossel had a pitch in the market, with clientele coming to see him there, where they were pleased to find a ready-to-wear collection suitable for their needs. The farmers came into town to trade, and although they often drank too much and got into fights amongst themselves, it was rare for them to pick on the Jews. In addition to this market trade, Harry's father had contracts with firms who needed the heavy fur-lined coats and other outer garments for their lorry drivers, or their drivers of horses and carts, who mostly worked in the open air. Another iron in the fire concerned his work for the TB sanatorium in Zakopane, up in the mountains. Before antibiotics and other advances in medication, it was the custom for people with tuberculosis to be treated by placing their beds outside in the fresh air, where they remained, even in the snow. Jossel made the warm fur-lined sacks for the sufferers to lie in.

In Poland before the war, when a deal was done, it was expected that the two parties would 'have a drink on it'. This drink was vodka. Jossel was not a drinker but had to imbibe for the sake of business as the customers expected it. Regular customers would come to the house, and Harry would be sent out for kosher sausages, which were always well liked. Harry also collected the empty vodka bottles and took them to a place that gave some money back on them which he was allowed to keep as a form of pocket money. Once, and only once, his father became tipsy, and the incident made a deep impression as it was so out of character. The local government had been selling off land at a knockdown price, and Jossel bought some on his own and some together with his brothers. Coming back from the council offices a bit the worse for wear, he asked Harry to bring him a coat so that he could go and sleep it off in the stables. When he went into the house to fetch the coat, Ruchel saw him and asked what he was doing. As soon as she discovered she went out and called for her husband to come in and to sleep it off inside. Harry understood that his father had been ashamed and had not wanted his wife to see him drunk, but Ruchel was not a superficial woman. She knew better than to imagine her husband was a drunkard and she grasped at once what must have happened.

Jossel was keenly interested in politics, and there was always political conversation going on at home. He was a Revisionist. Revisionists were followers of the Russian Jew Jabotinsky, who had become a Zionist after the Kishinev pogrom in 1903. In 1917 Jabotinsky had fought alongside General Allenby and had led the first crossing into Palestine, after which he was awarded the MBE by the British. In the 1930s, Jabotinsky became increasingly concerned about the deteriorating situation for Jews, especially the Jews in Poland, where he had most support, and he conceived a plan in 1936 to evacuate all the Jews of Poland, Hungary and Romania to Palestine. All three governments agreed, but the plan was rejected by the Polish Jews themselves, who felt that it 'played into the hands' of the many Polish antisemites. Fearing vicious Nazi pogroms, Jabotinsky issued an urgent warning to all the Jews of Europe in 1938, but he could not have envisaged the horror and almost total annihilation that was to come. Revisionists had uniforms and would march in the streets for part of their meetings, provoking laughter from some Polish onlookers. Their aim was to establish a Jewish State in Palestine, and long before the war Jossel talked frequently about emigrating to Palestine to live, free at last of all antisemitic persecution. In 1939, when there were rumours of a possible war, he went into Łódź to obtain visas but came back empty-handed. The price had shot up sky-high.

The *Rebbe* (pronounced 'Rebber', and the title for the Jewish spiritual leader in Tuszyn) lived almost next door to the Fuks and he was a very powerful man. What the *Rebbe* said 'went', and to a very great extent he ran the affairs of the Jewish part of the town. This rabbi was also a proficient businessman. He was tall and wore a *stramel* or long black 'Jewish' coat. Harry's father once had a dispute with him that was testament to Jossel's stature and integrity. What happened was swift but telling. Jossel was elected to become a *'dozzer'* or representative of the Jewish community on the Tuszyn town council. He received 111 votes, a number that Harry remembers distinctly. Jossel was highly respected, and his election must have been almost unanimous. The *Rebbe* had voted for him as well, but knowing Jossel had a reputation for 'being his own man', he wanted to make sure of his support in what he, the *Rebbe*, wanted. Immediately after the election, he asked Jossel to 'give him his hand' as a sign that he would never vote against him. Jossel resigned at once.

'If I give you my hand,' he said, 'I will only have one left, and what *good* will I be able to do with only one hand?!'

He was indeed his own person and refused to be the stooge of anyone.

Harry was a rambunctious child, however, and rebelled against his father. Jossel was very busy and did not always have time to explain things properly when he asked for something to be done. His youngest son would stick his chin out and simply not do what he was bid. This resulted in a hiding, usually administered with a whip, but the jobs were still not done. On one occasion Harry buried his father's cat o' nine tails in a field at the holiday resort of Tuszyn Las. On being asked for it sometime later, he got quite a bashing when it did not appear. He would have retrieved it, but he had forgotten where it was!

A very capable man, Jossel was skilled in many things. He played the violin well and as a young man had his own little Klezmer group that would provide the music for weddings. When he was older he dissolved this group as he was too busy, and only made music at home. On some Shabbas evenings Jossel would play his fiddle and Ruchel would sing, with friends and family coming round to the house to listen. In the winter months, when Jossel was especially busy, there would be no time for making music, as once the Sabbath was ended he would go straight back to work.

Jossel was very good with his hands, quite apart from tailoring. He had decided to build another house in their yard, at the bottom end of it, backing onto the street that was parallel to Remishfesvkego Street. The new house was one that he would let out for additional income. During the building of this house in their yard Harry saw his father argue with the builder, not liking the way a window had been put in. The builder refused to change it, so Jossel took over and installed the window correctly. At another time in the early 1930s he was involved in building the Tuszyn Sanatorium, when he and his brothers Lazer and Saul did all the glazing for its completely glass roof.

Harry's mother Ruchel (Plate 8) was a very different character and she always knew how to handle Harry and could make him do whatever she wanted. Whereas he was constantly in trouble with his father, when it came to his mother, who was gentle, persuasive, and kind, there was never any problem between them. Born Ruchla Gotesman in Sulejow, Poland, on 15 May 1904, she was the fourth child of seven children from her father's second marriage. Her family moved to Tuszyn when she was ten in August 1914, her father moving there with all the seven children from his second marriage. The youngest of her siblings, Bernard, was only three months old when they moved. Later, when in her teens, the story goes that she met Jossel because one of her friends was 'sweet' on him. This friend used to send Ruchel along to him with little messages.

After a time Jossel said, 'Stop bringing these messages. I don't want her, I want you.' She was twenty when they got married on 9 November 1924. [Plate 3]

Ruchel was a wonderful mother. Well educated and always well dressed, she was also a dressmaker and helped her husband in his workshop. She would embroider the 'Afghan' coats he made and do a variety of other useful jobs. In spite of her busy life she always had time for her children, looking after them and making sure they were clean and well cared for. An attractive and sophisticated woman, she was 'anybody's equal'. Full of life, she gave energy and a sense of wellbeing to her family.

The place of Ruchel's father, Harry's *Zaide*, his grandfather, was vital also (Plate 6). His first name was Wolf, like Jossel's father, but he was always called Welwol or Welwo. Reb Welwol Gotesman towered above other figures in Harry's childhood, outside of his immediate family, and this man remains to this day a source of wisdom and guidance. Harry was drawn to him and frequently went round to his house, never tiring of listening to his stories. Welwol, known with affection and respect by the courtesy title *Reb* (a title acknowledging the learning and wisdom of someone not a rabbi), was born in Sulejow to Uszer and Gitle Gotesman in about 1850, and he had six children from his first marriage, all of them boys. He had married very young, being only sixteen when his eldest son was born, not to mention the fact that he was already caring for a child as his first wife was a widow and brought a son with her when they married. Welwo's second wife may have been his first wife's cousin, or niece, as it was then considered better to marry a relative if there were previous children to mother. With his second wife Pawa (Plate 7) he was to have a further seven children, the youngest being Bernard, who was born when Welwo was sixty-six. People would tease him about having thirteen children.

'What do you *want* me to do with the wife?' he would reply. 'Beat her up?!'

This was all good-humoured banter, but people wondered 'how he had managed it' as the family slept together in one room. (See Gotesman family tree, Plate 36).

There was a chalk mine in Sulejow, and Reb Welwol made good use of it, dealing in chalk for the building industry. Chalk was an important material for builders as all the houses were whitewashed with it, and Grandfather would go directly to the mine, filling several large horse-drawn wagons to sell it wholesale. Once he had moved to Tuszyn, his chalk business became much smaller. In Tuszyn he set up house in Piotrków Gas (Gas = Street) and ran a restaurant there with the help of his wife Pawa, who did the cooking, and his daughter Devoira, who did all the other jobs a restaurant required. Once old age forced him to give up the restaurant he continued to trade in chalk, scaling down the business as time went on. Eventually, he sent Bernard with the wagon to Sulejow for supplies and confined his chalk-selling to Tuesdays, when he would sell small quantities to individuals from his wagon stall in the market. For the rest of the week the wagon was put away, being stored in or near the market.

Welwo was a tremendous teller of stories and he impressed his grandson greatly. He had all kinds of wise sayings and doings that are still remembered by Harry. One of these pearls concerned his philosophy of the market. If he had done well, he would walk home, 'so that his enemies would feel happy, but then so would he!' If he had done badly, he would hire a horse-drawn cab to make his enemies suffer, but he himself would be cheered up!

'Why should I be the only one unhappy?' he would say with a chuckle.

It is most doubtful that this grandfather had any enemies. He was well liked and respected by all. Welwo was wise as well as educated, and with his gift for telling stories he was a popular man. He was also a funny man with a great sense of humour, and he made others feel better after being with him. In his generation in Poland it was not usual for Jews to speak any language other than Yiddish, but he had a good command of Polish. Altogether, his grandson thought him glorious.

'Whenever I got into trouble', Harry would say, 'especially with my father for not doing what he told me to do, I would run to my grandfather before my father had a chance to give me a good hiding. When my father turned up angry, Grandfather would say, "Jossel, let's talk about it." My father, not being an evil person, would find his venom disappearing after a while. Thus, I avoided a hiding. I now realize, though, that the only way my father had to keep me in check was to give me a beating. I never remember my mother having to hit me. I think being beaten was not uncommon then and that also it was partly due to my father having so little time to explain things to me properly.'

Ruchel looked after her children and dressed them well. The boys wore shorts and always wore a *tzit-tzit* (pronounced 'sit-sit', ritual tassels, being a small version of the Jewish prayer shawl worn under their shirts) and a hat when outside. If they went to see their grandfather looking very clean and well turned out, he might say that they looked 'too good', and he would take a bit of soot from the oven and put a black mark on their noses, to 'keep off the evil eye'. This was less superstition than not wanting others to become jealous of them.

Reb Welwo was a truly religious person, with a small 'r'. He possessed a deep spirituality and had a large heart, observing religious customs without ever being a cold fanatic. Harry remembers being told on many occasions that they were related to the original and famous Gerrer Rebbe (Yitzchak Meir Alter, 1796–1866), and that this was something he should not forget. In other words, Grandfather was using the fact of their being related to this Hasidic leader from Ger in Poland as a source of pride, but in a way that said gently, 'Never forget who you are and of what faith.' Each weekday morning, Grandfather would leave his house and go out to pray. He never ate anything before he prayed, but Ruchel always made sure he had a warm drink afterwards, often sending her youngest son to stand outside the Beth Medrish (described later) with a glass of hot milk to be given to her father immediately after the service. Following the death of his second wife Pawa, Welwo moved from the large 'restaurant' house to a small place which was near his daughter Devoira, who would attend to his needs, going in to clean for him and do his washing. Now well into his eighties, he was looked after and fed by the three of his daughters, Devoira, Ruchel and Sura-Rachel, who had remained living in Tuszyn with their husbands and families. The sons from Grandfather's first marriage had dispersed around the country with their families and businesses, except for Beirech, who was still living in Sulejow. From the children of the second marriage, Chaim-Uszer, the third of the seven, had gone to live in Germany, moving on to France in 1922. He was the first of the family to leave Poland and was a tailor by trade, working at 173 Faubourg Saint-Antoine in Paris. Ruchel's eldest sister Esther-Guitel married a cousin, Henri Goldmyc. They had moved to France in 1924 (Plates 10 and 11), being followed there by Esther-Guitel's brothers Avrum and Bernard ten years later. Yitzchak, a grandson, went to Belgium with his father Moshe in the 1930s. Moshe was the youngest child from Grandfather's first marriage. Grandfather's children who left Poland for France and Belgium wanted to be more modern and achieve a higher standard of living than they were able to in Poland. They were also less religious than Reb Welwo.

Ruchel's sisters Devoira and Sura-Rachel (Plate 9) remained in Tuszyn after marriage, but Grandfather only went out to eat and 'be' in Ruchel's house. Devoira's house was always a bit of a mess, and her husband Gershon was not very religious. Gershon was a fishmonger, but following an accident he had lost an eye and was always referred to by everyone as 'One Eyed Gershon'. Remarkably, his fishmonger partner Avrum had also lost an eye, and they were a well-known pair. Sura-Rachel's husband Henutek was a barber and was not religious at all. It was for these reasons that Grandfather went to Ruchel's home rather than to the others, for although his son-in-law Jossel did not wear a beard, he was religious like Reb Welwo, and the atmosphere made him feel at home there. He always seemed to be in their house, certainly on Friday nights, when he would preside over the Sabbath meal. The home of Jossel and Ruchel Fuks was open house to him, and he visited frequently. They would hang onto every word he said, such was his stature and appeal. He was a great human being, and Harry considers that even now his influence stands him in good stead. He died in peace in 1938.

Harry remembers his grandfather's death vividly: 'He loved tinned sprats in oil, like sardines. Whenever I was in his house and he was eating some he'd always give me one. The day he died, I remember that he gave me the whole tin, and I knew he wasn't well. My Aunt Devoira who lived the nearest was there, too, as well as Aunt Sura-Rachel. Feeling unwell, Grandfather went to bed. My Aunt Devoira went to make him a glass of tea, and my other aunt Sura-Rachel went to fetch the doctor. In the meantime, Aunt Devoira took the tea to his bed and found him dead. He had died in the time it took to make the tea. I was there during all this and remember it. Although I loved him, at the age of seven or eight it was difficult to understand death, and I wasn't so sad. My cousin Esther, Aunt Devoira's daughter, was with me on that day also.'

Aunt Sura-Rachel and Henutek had a son soon after Grandfather's death and they named him Welwol.

Jona (Joino) Fuks, Harry's elder brother, was born on 2 February 1927, and the two boys were very close in spite of some usual sibling friction.

Harry recalls: 'My brother always gave the impression of being a bit sickly, and it seemed to me that he got more pampered than I and had more chocolates. I was hoping to be ill so that I could get more chocolate. My parents also said that Jona looked after his clothes better than I did. Being the eldest, all his clothes were new. Apart from at Rosh Hashanah (Jewish New Year) the clothes I got given were all hand-me-downs, which I hated. I didn't want to look after them; they were partly worn out already. My parents seemed to 'see' Jona more than me. I therefore decided not to eat one day, to make a point and get more attention like my brother did.

"I'm not eating it," I said.

My father asked, "Are you sure you don't want it?"

I replied "Yes!"

Father said, "We don't want to waste good food" and he asked me again if I was certain that I didn't want it.

I said again that I was certain. My father then took my food and ate it. Needless to say I never repeated this.'

Jona went up to the next stage of schooling before the war. This was a Polish, non-Jewish school. Antisemitism was quite pronounced there, and he was subjected to attacks, especially on the way home. The teachers knew about this and they could have stopped it, but they did nothing. The fights Jona got into were bad enough for him to need to take some pincers with him as a defensive weapon, and sometimes a family member would go and fetch him from school for protection.

Everybody grew sunflowers. On one occasion a fight had broken out between a group of young Christian and young Jewish boys. This meant that the Christian lads had gone there specifically to look for some Jewish boys to fight with; the Jewish youngsters did not go looking for trouble –

Before the War, Tuszyn, Central Poland, 1930–1939

they had enough anyway. Jona was part of this fight, and Harry spotted him, recalling to this day what happened:

'Being younger than the boys taking part and yet wanting to join in, I decided to get a dried and very hard sunflower stalk with the root ball still in place. I outflanked the Christian boys, going in behind them. This was childish and very silly, as after I'd walloped a few of them on the back of their heads, they turned on me and I had to be rescued by the Jewish boys. After this, though, I could join my brother's group. I had proved myself.'

It was the tradition in Jewish families then to name a child after a relative who had died. They did not name a child after a relative who was alive. Jona (Joino) and all the other Joinos on the Fuks side were named after the same person, great-grandfather Fuks. The Chaim-Uszers came from Harry's mother's family and were named after Great-Grandfather Uszer Gotesman, Reb Welwo's father.

Harry's sister, Rhuda-Pawa Fuks, was born in 1933. Her blonde hair and sweet features came with a loving heart, and she enhanced their home life with her good nature.

'Whereas it seemed I was always fighting with my brother,' remembers Harry, 'my sister was like a little angel. She always looked very pretty, with long blonde hair, and she was kind and generous too. When we were given chocolate, Jona and I would gobble it up quickly. She was slower to eat hers and would then share it with us.'

Harry Fox, Chaim Uszer Fuks, my husband, was born on 15 July 1930, and although he has an official paper to say that he is 'also known as' Harry Fox, he has never changed his name and never wishes to do so, continuing to use it on his passport and various other documents. At home in Poland he was always referred to as Chaim Uszer, both his names always said together as one, but written with no hyphen; and this is what I call him. He altered the spelling himself when writing to me, so that Uszer became Usher, but to most others he is Harry. Stubborn, intelligent and sometimes difficult, he revealed early on that he is a loyal person who does not hesitate to dive in to defend his own. Prickly and rebellious if not treated 'right', he would go to the ends of the earth for his mother and sister. A tough boy, his attraction to the wisdom, humour and stature of his grandfather betrays a greater depth and complexity of character. Harry reacts to people and events. This can be effective but can also land him in trouble! Blessed with a naturally positive disposition like his grandfather, however, he 'will not be kept down for long'.

The food and meals of home and childhood had meaning that was associated with ritual and the routine of daily life. Jossel usually got up at 5.00 am. Their house shared a party wall with the Beth Medrish, a prayer house which was not the main synagogue but a smaller additional place for weekday use. Jossel would listen out for the beginning of prayers next door. He would then join in at home, putting on *tefillin* (small leather boxes containing verses from the Torah, worn strapped across the forehead, arm and hand) to pray. Food for the soul came first, after which he had a snack of some bread, onion and tomato. He started work at 6.00 am. From 8.00 am until 9.00 am the family had breakfast, and Jossel would eat with them. In winter they had rice soup, a thin version of rice pudding, sweetened to keep out the cold. In summer, breakfast was rolls and butter, homemade yoghurt, tomatoes and cream cheese. The children always drank milk, and the parents drank lemon tea. The children came home from school for lunch. Suppers in the week consisted of either, potatoes and borscht, liver or beef stewed with sauce and potatoes, with homemade pickled cucumbers. Two large barrels stood in the passageway into their yard. One of these was for the borscht and the other for the pickled cucumbers.

The family did not have meat to eat every day, but Fridays were different. Lunch on Friday was always *krupnik*, a barley soup, followed by sugared buns. In the afternoon before the Sabbath came in, the family would have a bath in the portable *ballio*, and dress in good clothes. Sometimes on a Friday Jossel would take his sons to the *mikvah*. This was a place that contained the religious baths for men and, separately, for women. It also contained some baths that people were able to use to wash themselves in if they did not have anything such as a *ballio* to use at home. The man who ran the *mikvah* was paid very little and he had four children. Harry's family would pass their unwanted clothes on to him. This man also taught at *cheydah* (religion school) to supplement his income. The feast of the week was on Friday night, the Sabbath meal over which Grandfather would usually preside. After coming home from the service next door, Ruchel would light the candles, and her father said the blessings over the wine and *challah* (special bread). Then it was 'Food, glorious food'! Gefilte fish, chopped liver, chicken soup, chicken and vegetables were followed by puddings of apple purée, prunes and cooked pears. The meal ended with lemon tea and biscuits. The family employed a non-Jewish lady, a 'Shabbas Goy', who came in to light the fire for them at home, as they would not strike a match on the Sabbath.

It was after the Friday night meal that Jossel would sometimes question Harry about the week's Torah portion. This was the Bible passage allotted for the week, and Jossel had, after all, paid for him to attend *cheydah* and to be versed in its understanding. He would ask Harry to translate the passage from Hebrew into Yiddish and then explain its meaning. If, by some remote chance, Harry had not been diligent enough and studied as he should, if he stumbled over the words or was unable to interpret them, a right-hander was meted out. Jossel wanted his sons to be educated in their religion. He gave hard-earned money for the lessons and was more than disappointed if he felt it had been wasted. This early religious teaching has not been in vain, and Harry is now very grateful for it, being able to follow and join in services today, and recalling so much that makes sense of what it means to be Jewish.

If a stranger happened to be in Tuszyn on a Friday and was delayed there so that the Sabbath came in before they were able to travel home, they would be spotted at the Friday night service and always offered the hospitality of the Friday night meal and a bed for the night. Certainly, in small towns and villages this courtesy was general practice, and it was easy to carry out where everyone knew each other. It gave a sense of freedom and civility, for the stranger's family would know that if they did not return on a Friday they would be being looked after by another community, and in the age before telephones, this took away any worry. This behaviour brings to light the common bond and understanding between Jews, and those who offered hospitality on one occasion would know that if they were in a similar position elsewhere, the same consideration would be given to them.

The Saturday mornings of the Sabbath were also different. The adults had no breakfast. They did not eat before praying, and on Saturday the family walked to the main synagogue at the end of their street. This synagogue was in fact only opened up once a week on Saturdays, or for the High Holy Days of Rosh Hashanah and Yom Kippur. The Beth Medrish was used during the week, which included being the venue for the Friday night service. One of Uncle Lazer's sons, Uszer, possessed a beautiful voice and was a very talented singer. He led the singing in the synagogue and was also in charge of the synagogue choir. The service took some time, and Harry would usually go outside and play in the synagogue grounds, an activity thankfully permitted, strict attendance at the service not being required until the age of thirteen. After the family returned from the synagogue a large pot was collected from the bakery. Each family would take their pot of food to the bakery on Friday, where it was left to cook in the warm oven overnight. This arrangement meant that they did not have to cook at home on the Sabbath. In the pots was *chulent*, a mixture of fatty beef, potatoes, butter beans and barley. Another compartment in the same pot was full of a kind of cake made from sweet dough and called *kiegel*. The family name of the baker they went to was Jacobovitch, and he lived in the Fuks' original smaller house, which he had bought from them. The bakery was in Kościelna (Church) Street, and the premises were rented from Jossel's cousin, whose surname was Goldberg. This Goldberg's son, another Harry, came to England before the war. (After the war he heard from relatives in France that Jona and Harry had survived, and he and his wife Annie would often invite the two boys for meals, especially on Friday nights. They kept in touch until Harry and Annie died. The Harry of *this* story paid for that Annie's funeral.) For supper on Saturday nights, when the Sabbath was over, the family would eat a meal that was quick and easy to prepare consisting of boiled potatoes with the traditional *schmaltz* herring.

The Fuks children were never given shop-bought toys; they made their own. Harry was talking about this once when his youngest daughter Lucy was three or four years old, and children 'always listen'. Lucy left the room, came back with her favourite toy and gave it to her father.

One successful toy Harry made as a child was a train with carriages. The wheels were made from discarded cotton reels with their tops and bottoms cut off. Bits of wood and cardboard created the carriages, and the train engine was the mechanism from an old clock. He recalls: 'One of my cousins, the son of my father's only sister Sara, was an adult and he showed me how to use the clock's works to enable the train to move. The train's shape was built up over the workings, and once wound up, it pulled the train along. A wonderful toy to have! I got the mechanism by swapping it with a school friend for three razor blades. When he saw what I had done with it he wanted it back and he grabbed it and ran off. I chased him and we had a fight. I came home with my train engine.'

There were plenty of grassy spaces in Tuszyn, and football was played a lot. Jona and Harry each played with boys their own age. On Saturdays, after the family had attended the main synagogue, where the formal service lasted for at least two hours, they went home for lunch, but at certain times of the year the boys were sent out again, to their religion schoolteacher in the afternoon. Sometimes this was simply too much to bear, and they skived off to play football. On one such Saturday Harry wore new shoes. He took them off for playing as football would scuff them and he would be in trouble for that, not to mention having dodged religion school. At the end of the game the new shoes could not be found! The boys searched and searched. Harry was afraid to go home and face his father. The memory of what did happen next has gone.

One of Jossel's elder brothers, Uncle Lazer, had a goat he kept for milk, and he considered that the milk from his goat was superior to that on offer from the daily milk cart. Harry and his friends would sneak in and milk Lazer's goat before he got to her. Needless to say, this uncle would be most upset at finding no milk in his beautiful goat! He never did realize why she was such a bad milker. Harry went to Uncle Lazer's house a lot as his youngest son Uszer was near to him in age.

Nathan was a great-uncle on the Fuks side, and the dairy Harry's family went to was in part of his property which he rented out to his brother Isaac. Anszel, Jossel's youngest brother, with his wife Rojza-Perla and their children, rented living accommodation there as well. Nathan was very fit and healthy, and at the age of ninety-nine he carried a sack of earth on his back for two miles, in order to renew his earthen floor before the festival of Pesach. He had a large pear tree by his house which produced small sweet pears. Harry and others would try and pinch them, but Nathan would chase them off with vigour! It took the Nazis to kill him.

There was still some family living in Suleyow, and Harry was sent there to stay with his Uncle Beirech. Beirech was the eldest child of Grandfather Gotesman's first marriage, and his trade was making saddles, bridles and general harness for horses. He had in fact made the cat o' nine tails for Jossel, the one that Harry had buried and lost. Jossel had asked him to make it for him and the handle was the leg bone of a deer. Beirech was well liked by everyone and was the kind of man people came to for advice. People also asked for his help in disputes, and Beirech often acted as a mediator. Harry recalls travelling to Suleyow in their own horse and cart, for the days of working horses were far from over. Uncle Beirech had three children, two sons Uszer and Froïm and a daughter who married a rabbi.

Harry never met his other uncles from Grandfather Gotesman's first marriage except for Moshe, Yitzchak's father, but he did not meet him until after the war. Beirech's brother Schmil was the only one of them to have been in the Army. He was a soldier for a time in the Caucasus and was in Tashkent when he met his wife. They later settled in Łódź, where Schmil worked as a baker, gaining a reputation for being impeccably well dressed and always wearing a rose in his buttonhole. Schmil died very soon after his father and was in fact the same age as his father's second wife, Pawa. Menil was also a baker and lived in Warsaw. Leibich had lived in Łódź but he died very young after being married for just a month. His early death was due to an infection following the extraction of a tooth.

David, one of Beirech's brothers, had been living in Warsaw. He escaped the Holocaust by being out of the country, having run away to South America with another woman before the war, abandoning his wife and his five children. His wife was unable to support her five children on her own, so other relatives helped out, taking in a child each. Meyer, the youngest, went to live with Harry's family, and Jossel was going to teach him the tailoring trade, but the arrangement did not last very long. Meyer refused to pray, and Jossel told him to leave his house, whereupon he returned to Warsaw, and they lost touch with him until after the war. Meyer had fled to Russia before the Warsaw Ghetto was sealed, becoming the only one of David's family to survive, but it was not until the 1960s that father and son saw each other again. Meyer had married Miriam whilst still in Russia, and they had lived in both Germany and Israel before moving to the United States with their two children, Leila and Victor. Leila was getting married, and Meyer knowing his father's address in South America, wrote to invite him to the wedding. David came, but understandably their meeting was not easy.

Whilst Harry was always at home for meals, he sometimes arrived at a relative's house just when they were going to eat, and he was always invited to join them. An extra meal was very acceptable to an energetic lad! One aunt, Aunt Chaia, was married to the Uncle Lazer of goat fame. She was not the greatest of housekeepers, and her plates were very broken and in short supply. A traditional meal would be made up of half a plate of mashed potato and half of borscht. It took skill to keep a broken plate tilted to prevent the borscht from running off it. All the same, it was wonderful for Harry to feel part of such a numerous and welcoming family. There was always somewhere to go and someone to play with. Chaia and Lazer had four children, their fourth being Uszer the singer, who was Jona's age. Joino, their third child, had the distinction of being a member of the Tuszyn town football team. He was the only Jewish player in the team, being too good at the game to ignore, in spite of the fact that Jews were not normally included.

Isaac Fuks was an uncle of Jossel's and he had a dairy, the one rented from his brother, Harry's Great-Uncle Nathan. After Isaac died, the dairy continued to be run by his widow, and she gave Harry meals there too. The dairy couple had a son also called Joino, who was Jossel's first cousin. This Joino was a tall man, good looking and very strong. He was known by everyone as 'the strongest man in Tuszyn'. If there was a scrap between children, one child might say, 'I'll go and get my father' or 'I'll fetch so and so.' If, however, someone threatened to 'go and get Joino' there was an immediate end to any squabble. A physically powerful person, Joino was very gentle by temperament and never used his strength in any way except for the defence of others. For example, on market day in Tuszyn there were a few occasions when incomers began to pick on some of the ultra-Orthodox Jews. These people were not equipped for fighting, and Joino would swiftly put a stop to it, taking on the role of a guardian. Harry witnessed him seeing off a couple of Poles who were attacking some Jewish men who wore *payot* (side curls) and the traditional long black coats. Amongst the young men of the Jewish community in Tuszyn there were some who wanted a trial of strength with Joino, wishing to test out his legendary brawn in the hope of perhaps being able to take away his crown as the strongest man. Not one of these hopefuls ever succeeded. Joino had a son, Isaac, named after his grandfather, who had died a year or two before his birth. Joino's little Isaac must have been born in 1938.

One more of Jossel's brothers, and next to him in age, was Saul. He had been sent to Austria to be educated and was blessed with handsome film star good looks. He was one of the Jewish representatives in the Tuszyn local government and made many non-Jewish friends. Some of these became friends of Harry's family also, and he remembers sitting on the knee of a policeman visiting the house. A tailor by trade, Saul was a business partner of his brother Lazer. They shared a house and a workshop, making off-the-peg clothes.

Jossel's sister Sara had one son who was a cavalry officer in the Polish Army, and Harry remembers his sword. For him to have attained the rank of officer was most unusual for a conscript, let alone a Jew, and it was said that he 'was the pride of the regiment'.

Haircuts were popular, for another uncle, Ruchel's brother-in-law, was the barber Henutek. Whenever Harry went to him for a trim he would always slip some money into his nephew's hand. After ten generations of Fuks living there, and then Gotesmans, relations were all around, and front doors everywhere belonged to family. There were cousins in the street to play with and older ones to welcome and look out for him, as well as numerous uncles and aunts. This gave Harry a deep sense of security and of belonging and contributed to the happiness and wellbeing of his childhood. Weddings were times of great joy and celebration as well as tremendous fun. The *chuppa* (canopy held over bride and groom at Jewish weddings) was frequently set up in the street, where there was dancing and the wedding feast. After dark on wedding nights the children would run about with flaming torches made from besom brooms soaked in oil.

School was very close by, next door in fact, being in the yard of the Beth Medrish. As a Jewish school, Yiddish was used for religious studies and Polish for the Polish curriculum. School began at nine, with lunch at midday, which was eaten at home. Afternoon school lasted until supper at five. On Mondays and Thursdays, it was back to school after supper, to *cheydah*, for additional religious teaching. This went on from six until nine at night. On Fridays, school finished at lunchtime. The teacher in *cheydah* was very boring and he neglected his duties. Setting his pupils a task, he would then take out his false teeth, put them on the table and rest his head there. Sleep followed quickly. The head of this pedagogue rested on the table and his long beard flowed across it. What was a small boy to do? Little bits of paper were torn up, drawing pins collected, and the beard was pinned to the table.

This same teacher had a cat o' nine tails and often used it to beat his students. One day, the students got together and destroyed it by rubbing garlic into the leather thongs, which then went rotten and dropped off. On one occasion, Harry had a fight with a boy, and the teacher chased him. He went home and the teacher followed, wanting to beat him there and then.

To Harry's astonishment Jossel said, 'Tell me what he's done and I'll do it.'

Harry suddenly realized that although his father beat him himself, he *was his father* and would also look after him. This incident made a profound impression and gave Harry a different perspective on things.

Harry was a bit wild at school and had his share of fights, but he enjoyed it nonetheless. He was especially skilful at maths, which he liked the best because he was good at it and it was taught by a nice lady teacher who suited him. Harry's best friend from school was called Ozier. Later, they went through the war together, Ozier surviving, but they lost touch after Ozier joined the navy in Israel.

Individuals and entire families were frequently referred to by nicknames rather than their family names. These names could last a short time following a particular incident, or stick and become more permanent. The Fuks family were referred to as the 'Paints' ('Stomachs') due to Jossel's mother often buying tripe, which was cheap, to feed her large family. Another family had a more unfortunate name of the *Parechs* ('Scabs'), a Yiddish word which conjures up heads covered in itchy quantities of them. Then there were the 'Horse Thieves', and a man known as the Town *Grepser*, literally the Town Burper, who could belch to order for children if they gave him an apple! One man who had been bitten on his rear by a dog was subsequently known as 'Half Arse'. A very religious bearded fellow was owed some money by a Polish farmer. The farmer had no money to pay him with so gave him a pig instead! The man was seen walking through Tuszyn with this pig on a rope. He was obviously going to sell it, but the name 'Pig Herder' stuck thereafter, an unusual name indeed for a very observant Jew. The *Krupniks* were a big family of large, well-built people; their nickname came from the goodly pot of *krupnik* that they always had on the go.

Harry loves holidays and revels in new places, new people and new experiences, but he always wants to come home. When he was a child, school was out for more than three months in the summer. This may seem a long time, but they had no other breaks at all, not even during the freezing winter. Jossel always had several businesses on the go, and with two of his brothers, Lazer and Saul, and with Jossel 'as the brains', an apartment block was built in the Forest of Tuszyn. Jossel traded coats that he had made in exchange for the building's bricks. This holiday resort was essentially for the people of Łódź, and it consisted of about twenty apartment blocks. The Forest of Tuszyn, called Tuszyn Las, was ten miles from the centre of Łódź. (Tuszyn itself being twelve miles away.) There was a man-made lake in the forest for swimming and boating, and the good people of Łódź would rent an apartment there for the whole summer vacation. The apartments were of a very simple design, having one big room, a kitchen and a veranda. As far as Harry remembers, the flats had no lavatories. Harry's family moved to the resort for the summer as a business venture. Initially, they lived in their own apartment block, where they had also opened a shop selling necessities of every kind. Their store sold everything the holidaymakers could ever want, from food to coal, and even medicine. There was little tailoring work to be had in the summer, so the store was the work, and it was the job of Jona and Harry to deliver the goods to the various families. This was the online delivery service of the day, but Harry disliked having to carry the heavy coal upstairs for customers. Later on, Jossel purchased additional land and built another place for them to live, with a new shop attached. It was big enough for them to employ a woman living with them as a helper. The old shop and apartment were rented out. During the week, mostly women and children stayed in the forest, as the menfolk remained in town for work, only coming at the weekends. In order to replenish the store, Jossel and one of his sons would drive their horse and cart the two miles back to Tuszyn for supplies. On Friday mornings Jona and Harry would go about with a tank of live carp on the cart, selling fish. Jossel had also used his tailoring skills to set up this venture, exchanging cloth car coats for the live carp! This assignment was finished by lunchtime, when the horse and cart became a taxi service for the men joining their families at the weekend. Passengers were picked up from the Tuszyn Las tram stop, which was called Palestinka. This stop was the nearest one to the Fuks' apartment block, but there were other tram stops in the resort. The boys were allowed to keep the money they earned from this taxi work, and in the year before the war they were both saving up to buy bicycles. Jossel took their money 'for safe keeping', but then found he needed it and used it for more essential things. Jona and Harry never got their bikes.

When Harry was seven or eight he asked his father to teach him to swim. Jossel's method was to throw him into the lake! Harry knew his father would not let him drown, and following a bit of a struggle he did learn. Jossel liked to swim, too, and would go in after work in the afternoon.

In winter, the lake had another use. The Fuks were not there, but they saw the results in the summer. Frozen lake water was chopped up into blocks of ice, which were then heaped up into icy mountains. These were covered with sawdust to prevent them melting, and in the summer the ice was sold to keep food cool. Tuszyn Las, so thriving and full of people in the summer, was, apart from the ice-choppers, completely empty in winter.

In the summer of 1939, the threat of war hung over everyone and the holidaymakers went back to their homes earlier than usual.

Chapter 3

The War

Just before the German invasion of Poland, the Tuszyn town council ordered all its inhabitants to paint their houses on the outside in the vain hope that if they looked good, the Germans would not destroy them. Poland fought. Polish fighters were brave but ill-equipped, and in some battles they were driven to attack the most up-to-date German tanks from horseback. People were leaving and going to Russia for safety, and when they heard the noise of the guns in Tuszyn, Jossel decided that it was time to leave also and take the family east towards Russia, at least whilst the battle for Poland was going on. They set out, but after travelling a short distance Jossel changed his mind.

'Where are we running to?' he asked.

Jossel's thoughts were that they would not know anyone in Russia, or even find a roof over their heads, and they returned home. Not long afterwards, Harry remembers seeing the retreating Polish Army coming through the town, bringing their cows, large numbers of cows, with them. One Polish officer shot himself there.

Jossel's youngest brother Anszel did leave for Russia at this time, but he made his escape alone and left his wife and children behind. This was a terrible thing to do. Years later, when Harry was dealing with manufacturers in America, there always seemed to be a Holocaust survivor in the sample rooms. Through talking and comparing notes over several visits, the name of an Anszel Fuks who had survived in Russia came out. Further investigation revealed that it must indeed be Jossel's youngest brother, and an American survivor gave Harry his address in Israel. Harry went there to find him, and by coincidence Jona was in Israel at the same time. A friend took them round to the address they had been given and they met his wife, who said that Anszel was out. Getting the telephone number, the brothers rang it in the evening, but Anszel, now in his eighties, refused to see them or even admit that he was their uncle. He was too ashamed to face them.

* * *

German scouts soon roared into Tuszyn on their motorbikes. The scouts were quite friendly and some of them gave out sweets to the children. Within days, though, Germans filled Tuszyn and took it over, immediately ordering restrictions and hardships on all Jews. No Jews were allowed to go to school. (Harry, having been nine in July, did not mind this at first.) Every Jew had to wear the Star of David at all times. No Jew was permitted to attend synagogue, and so on. This synagogue order was relaxed for one day when a film crew arrived. On this day a number of mainly elderly Jews were forced to go the synagogue to be actors in a cynical pretence aimed to show the world that 'Jews could still go and pray'. The film did not reveal how these 'actors' were abused during this charade. Harry was looking on and witnessed the agony of a man having his beard set on fire. Tuszyn, being a small place, was not always troubled so directly, and the mass of Germans moved on to their next conquest. They had bigger fish to fry, but there were still many beatings of Jews and constant verbal abuse from the Germans who had remained and who were now running the town. Jews were barred from walking on any pavement; they had to walk in the road, but some freedom of movement

1. The two brothers, Jona and Harry, c.1933.

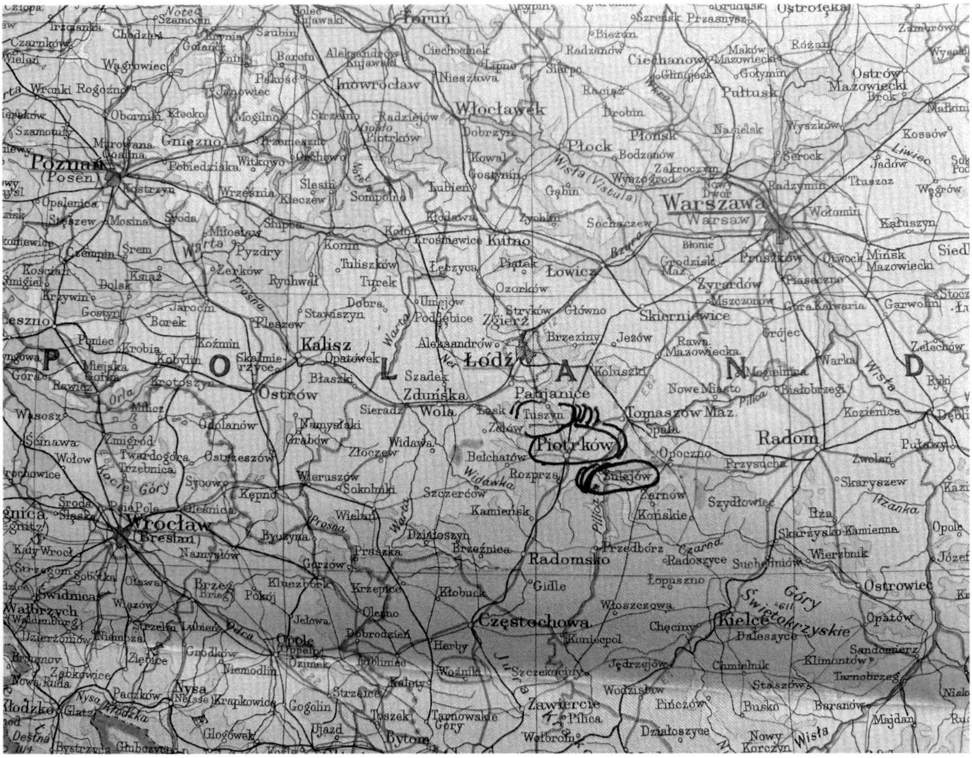

2. Map showing location of Tuszyn, Central Poland.

Skorowidz aktów ślubu za 1924

d. koly	Nazwiska i imiona nowoże...
1	Arer Moszek = Blum Ajdla
2	Birnbaum Chil = Hampel Udela
3	Cała Josek = Cała Fajga
4	Finkiel Gerszon = Golerman Dwojra
5	Fisz Srmul Majer = Morkowicz Hana
6	Fuks Josek = Golerman Ruchla
7	Jakubowicz Ajzyk Dawid = Cała Srojndla Fa...
8	Hartman Srulim Majer = Lasman Zysla
9	Lachman Nachman = Szwarc Blada Mal...
10	Niechcicki Wigdor Wolf = Obarzanek Blu...
11	Piotrkowski Manel = Szwarc Hana Rojza
12	Obarzanek Jcek Lajwel = Rozencwajg Cyr...

3. Marriage Register: Harry's parents.

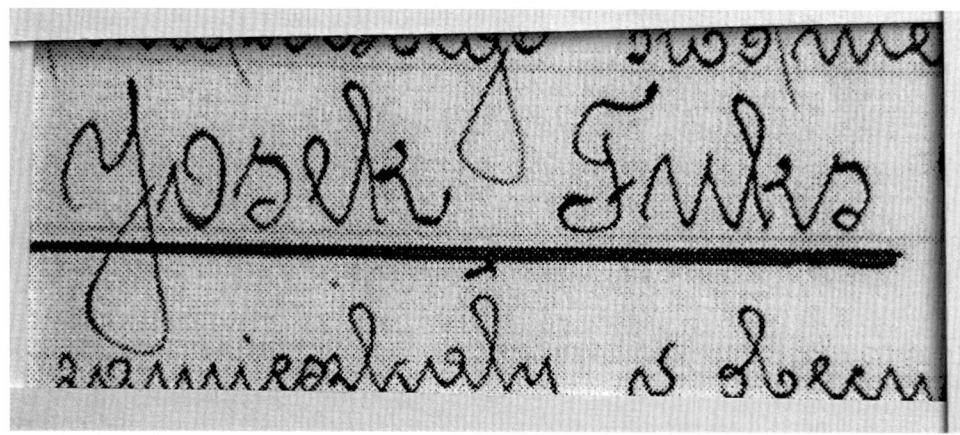

4. Signature of Josek Fuks (Jossel).

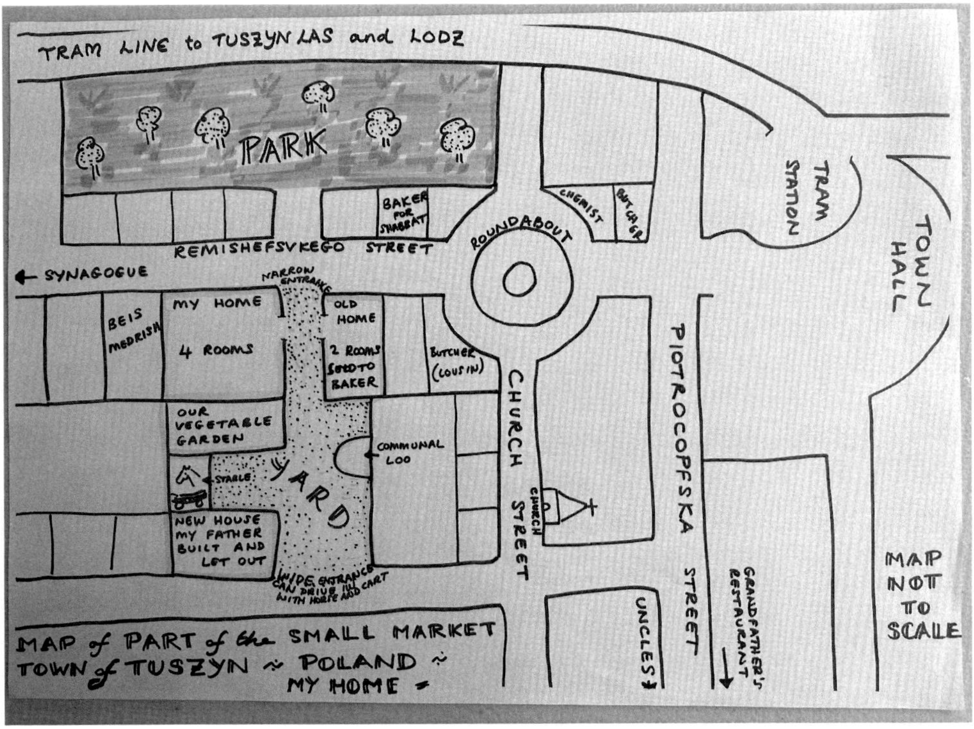

5. Hand-drawn map: part of Tuszyn showing Harry's home(s), Church Street (Ulica Kościelna in Polish).

6. Maternal grandfather Wolf Gotesman.

7. Maternal grandmother Pawa Gotesman.

8. Ruchla Fuks (Ruchel), Harry's mother.

9. Aunt Sura-Rachel.

10. 1924: standing Ruchel: L-R Rose, Leon, Aunt Esther-Guitel, baby Pauline.

11. Standing: Uncle Chaim-Uszer: L-R Leon, Uncle Henri Goldmyc, Pauline, Aunt Esther-Guitel, Rose (established in France).

8.	Fuks Calel	15/10 1924.	Piłsudskiego 10.	23 b 23 a⁴
9.	Fijołek Józef	1/12 1926.	Topolowa 6.	23 a⁷
10.	Filinger Michał	19/8 1926.	Piłsudskiego 45.	23 B.
1.	Fidala Józef	17/1 1928.	Karolińowska 23.	23 a⁴ 23 b
2.	Fuks Jojne	2/2 1927.	Zamurowa 10.	14 c.

12. Joino (Polish spelling on list): Jona's name on Hortensia Glass Factory list.

	...warol	1927		
9	Fligiel Wacław	2.1. 1929	Dąbrowska 14	23 a⁴
20	Fuks Chaim	15.7. 1930	Zamurowa 10	23 b
1.	Figa Józef	1.12. 1928	Krinski Rynek 8.	4 c 6
2	Frydman Tadeusz	2.8. 1926	Ziem lorch 40	5 n+6
3	Fraczkowski Czesław	9.9. 1925	Ziem lorch 107	21 f
4	Finkelsztajn	19.12		

13. Chaim Fuks: Harry's name on Hortensia Glass Factory list.

14. 1997 official certification: Harry employed full-time in Hortensia Glass Factory (slave labour for all Jews post-9/11/1942).

15. 1945 post-war: Czechoslovak police document showing Harry's DoB as 1931 (to assist Jona coming to the UK).

Lékařský záznam.						(31) DODATEČNÝ ZÁZNAM
1.	2.					Dočasné potvrzení totožnosti vydané:
(25) Datum odhmyzení		Způsoby				
(26) Zdravotní stav při příchodu		(27) Záznamy o očkování				Číslo datum podpis úřadu
		Druh	Dávka	Datum	Značka	
		T.	1.			Fuks Chaim
POZNÁMKY			2.			
			3.			2.Kl.Volksschule
		D.	1.			
			2.			1939 Piotrkow Ghetto
		T.T.	1.			Czestochowa A.L.
			2.			Buchenwald K.L.
			3.			Dora K.Z.
		O.				Northausen K,Z.
		S. Vacc.	Datum	Značka	Reakce I V VA	Harcung K.L.
						Litomarzyce K.L.
Lékařská prohlídka při příchodu:		(28) Konečná lékařská prohlídka:				Budziejewice K.L.
Datum				Datum		zuletzt Theresienstadt
						Eltern: Fuks Josek Schneider
lékař		lékař				Fuks Ruchla geb. Potersman
(29) Povolení odchodu nebo visum		(30) Záznam přijímacího střediska				Vater umgekommen
						Mutter und Schwester verschleppt und
						verschollen

16. 1945 post-war: (cover photograph) Czechoslovak list of Ghetto/Camps Harry was in.

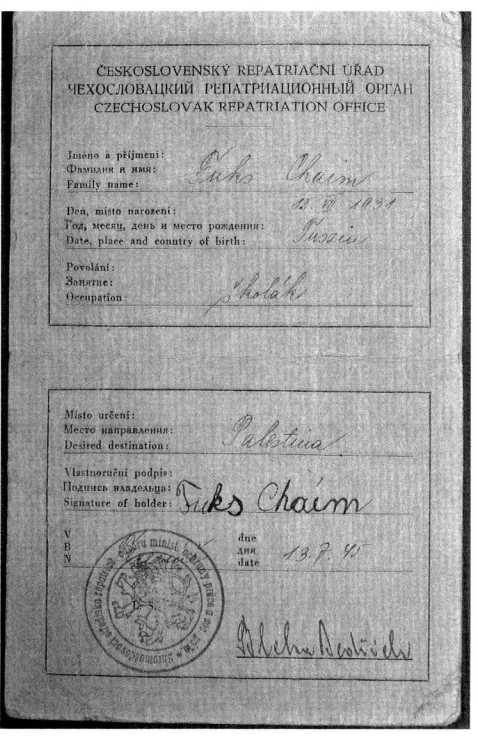

17. 1945 post-war: Czechoslovak Repatriation Document showing Harry had originally wanted to go to Palestine.

18. Prague, August 1945. Harry second left.

19. English lesson, Windermere. Harry partly obscured behind boy on right of bench.

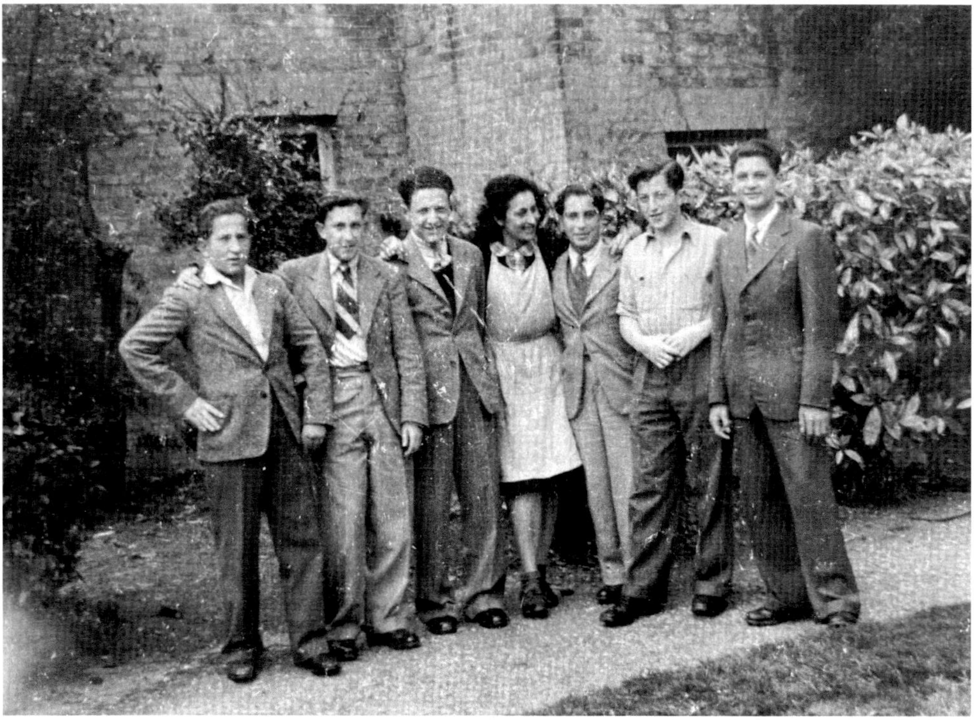

20. Loughton Hostel. Harry far left with 'Boys' and Reuma.

INTER - OFFICE - COMMUNICATION

MEMORANDUM

Reference No. 25th July 1946

From Miss Black To Miss Fellner

re Chaim FUKS, DP.64

Herewith Landing Slip in respect of the above, on which the birth date has been altered by the Police to 15.7.1930. The card is already with you.

Gwen Black

1876

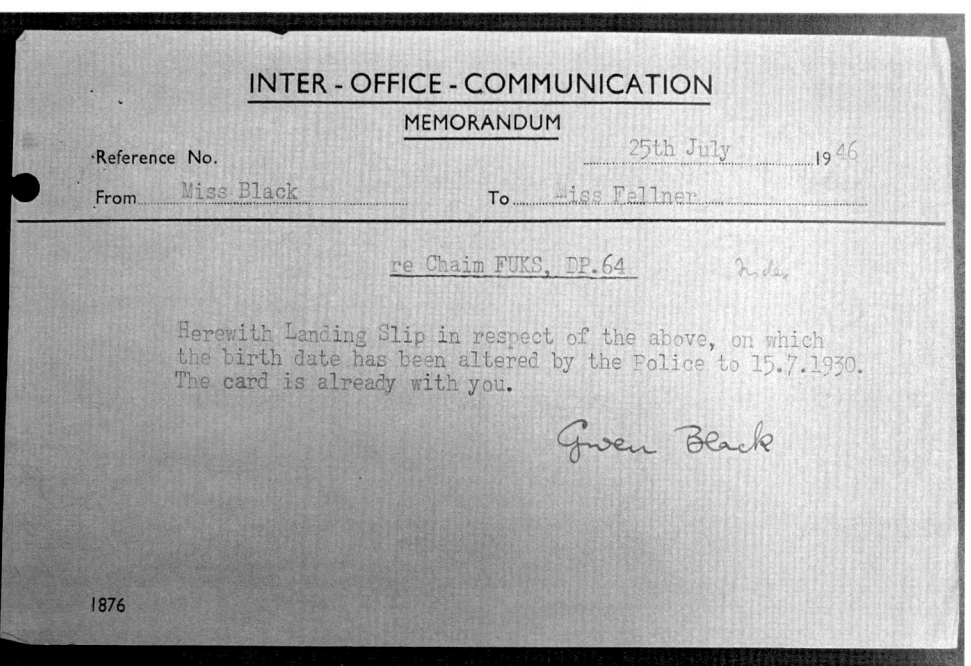

21. 1946. CBF memo re UK police correcting Harry's DoB back to 1930.

22. 1946 Holocaust Survivors march in London. Harry was there but not in the photo.

23. Aunt Esther-Guitel/Uncle Henri Goldmyc's Paris restaurant letter head.

24. Yitzchak Gotesman, Brussels.

25. The 'Boys' football team, Hackney Marshes, 1947. Harry kneeling second row left.

26. 'His own boss'!

27. Harry's garment labels: his own design.

28. A fine young man.

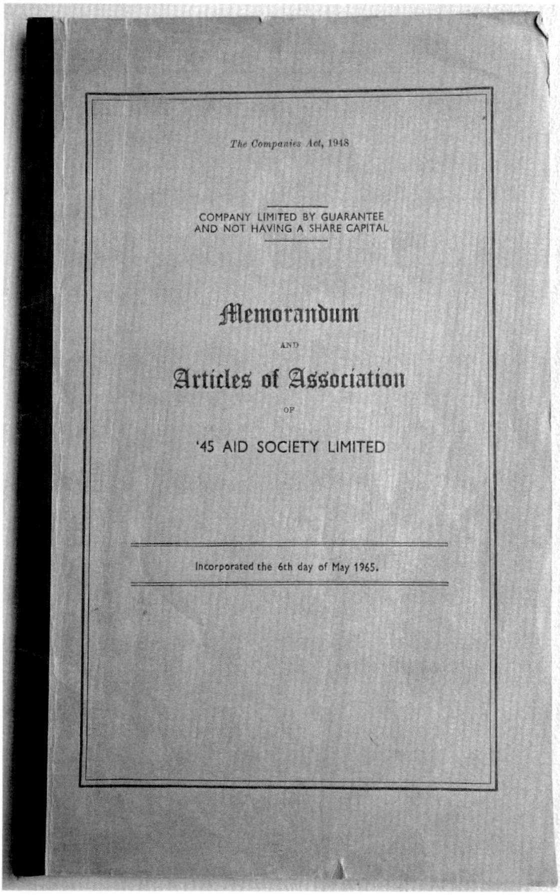

29. Cover of original Articles of Association, '45 Aid Society.

30. 50th Anniversary of Liberation: '45 Aid Society Annual Reunion, 1995.

31. Harry with Queen Elizabeth II: UK first Holocaust Memorial Day, 2005 (photographer unknown).

HOLOCAUST
MEMORIAL DAY
Admit
Mr Harry Fox
Room
Throne Room Group 1
To a Reception to mark
Holocaust Memorial Day 2005
at St James's Palace, SW1
on Thursday, 27 January 2005, arrival time from 10.00am
Please present this card on arrival

HOLOCAUST
MEMORIAL DAY
In the Gracious Presence of Her Majesty The Queen
The Secretary of State for the Home Department
requests the pleasure of the company of
Mrs Annie Fox
at the Holocaust Memorial Day 2005 National Event at Westminster Hall, Palace of Westminster
on Thursday, 27 January 2005, from 2.30pm to 3.30pm
Dress: Lounge suit/Day dress
Entrance: To be admitted at Carriage Gates
Doors will open at 12.00pm and close at 2.00pm precisely **Please present this card on arrival**

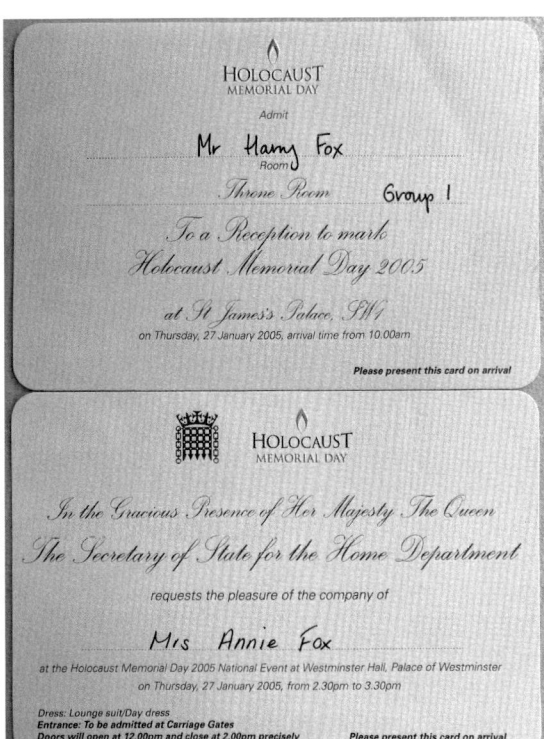

32. Tickets for UK first Holocaust Memorial Day.

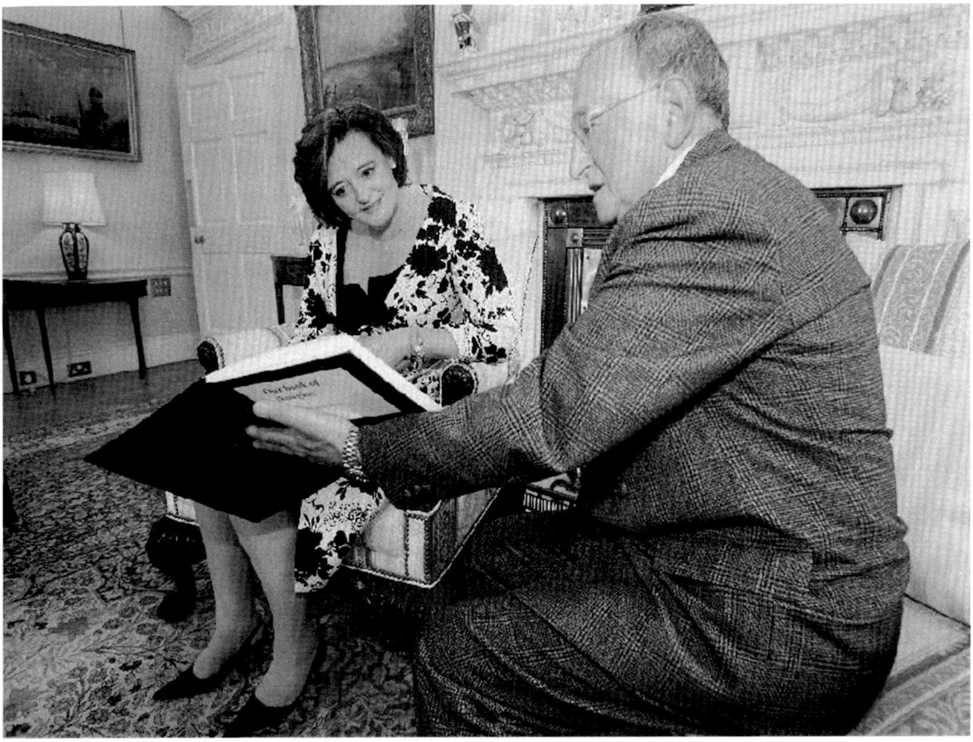

33. Harry with Cherie Blair at Number 10: showing her letters from schools (photographer unknown).

Modern History Review

in conjunction with

The Ridings High School

"FASCISM IN EUROPE"

10.00 am	Jonathan Osmond	
	Professor of Modern European History	
	University of Wales Cardiff	
Lecture:	'Fascism, Its Nature, Appeal and Imagery'	
10.55 ~ 11.10 am	Break	
11.10 am	Professor Richard Overy	
	Department of History	
	Kings College London	
Lecture:	'Weimar Germany and the Rise of Nazism'	
12.10 pm	Harry Fox	
Lecture:	'The Holocaust' : A talk by a survivor	
12.55 ~ 2.00 pm	Lunch	
2.00 pm	Donald Cameron Watt	
	Professor Emeritus of International History	
	London School of Economics	
Lecture:	'Hitler ~ Accident or Design? Hitler and his opponents in German History'	
3.00 pm	Mrs Sally Waller	
	AEB History Examiner	
Lecture:	'Answering 'A' Level Questions'	
3.50 pm	END	

34. Poster for talk, Harry and professors.

was still possible, and Harry recalls going to Łódź with his mother once or twice in order to take food to relatives who were already going short.

On 30 November 1939, at two o'clock in the black small hours of the morning, at the time when everyone was fast asleep in their beds, hordes of Germans poured into Tuszyn. They raced around banging on doors, and the soldiers began screaming and shouting that all Jews had two hours in which to leave town or be shot. Gunfire tore the night as the Nazis fired continuous warning salvos into the dark air. The Germans burst into Jossel and Ruchel's house, shrieking and yelling, making quite sure that their orders were understood. The shock and terror of this moment can barely be imagined, and after over seventy years Harry can 'still hear' the sound of the German jackboots on the wooden floors of his lovely home.

Jossel and Ruchel organized everything. They took their horse and cart and put what they could into the cart. They then took some things out of the cart – to make room for Jossel's tailoring machine. Jossel was able to think, and to think of how to work and keep his family, even at such a terrible moment.

* * *

After over ten generations there, this is how, in the dead of a winter's night, Harry and his family and his extended family, together with all the other Jews of Tuszyn, left their homes and their home town – for ever.

The Tuszyn Jews were told to go to the town of Piotrków Trybunalski, which was about the same distance away as Łódź. The night was freezing cold and the temperature was noted by some as being minus 20°C. Jossel wisely *insisted* that the family must walk rather than ride on the cart, in order to try and keep themselves warm. This was sagacious indeed, as it is recorded that several children froze to death before reaching Piotrków. On arrival there it was still dark, but they were met by some Jewish community leaders, who allocated temporary accommodation. Harry's family were sent to a room which they had to share with two other families, but as they had travelled together and arrived together, the other two families belonged to Jossel's brothers Lazer and Saul. Altogether there were fifteen of them, and they spent the remainder of the night attempting to sleep on the floor. Without knowing it, they were now in the first Jewish Ghetto set up by the Germans in Poland. The order for this Ghetto to be created had been issued by the city commissar, Oberburgermeister Hans Drexel, on 8 October 1939.

On the following day the family was given a room to themselves. This room was upstairs, above a Polish linseed oil factory which was still in operation, and the family that lived across the landing was not Jewish. The Ghetto was simply a district of Piotrków chosen from a few of its streets where Jews had predominated, but where Poles had been living side by side with them as well. The Germans had marked out this area within which to contain all the Jews cleared from the surrounding towns and villages. Later on, when the Ghetto was closed, all the Poles had left, and it contained only Jews. The house Harry found himself in lay between Samorowa Street, Kościelna Street and the Yiddish Gas. The main entrance to the house was in Kościelna Street, where imposing doors opened onto a passage into a courtyard, with the dwelling beyond. (This passage was used subsequently by Harry and a boy he had become friendly with, as a means to settle accounts. A large Polish boy who was a bit older than they were had been picking on them repeatedly. This particular boy used to shout abuse at them, try to hit them and generally cause them trouble. Harry and his new friend decided to do something about it, challenging their tormentor and luring him into the passage. The friends had worked out a plan of action. The friend ran ahead as if running away from the thug, provoking a chase, and once they were both in the passage, Harry, who was waiting for this moment, closed the large doors. Sandwiched between the two knights, the bully came off the worse for wear and did not cause trouble again.) There was a back door to this house also, and this led into Samarova Street.

In the beginning, whilst the Ghetto was still open, Poles came in and out all the time, trading with the Jews, and some lived and worked there as before. On his first morning in Piotrków Harry went out to roam around his new habitat and meet the local boys and gangs. The world had opened up a bit for him, and he had come into a much larger environment with many more people. That very first day he discovered some lads playing *dwaognia*, a game using a football that is thrown rather than kicked. He wanted to join in, but one of the group named Kojol (who is still alive today and living in Florida) wasn't keen to let him in, and they had a punch-up. Some of the lads began to help Kojol, making it an unfair fight. Another boy who happened to be looking on saw what was happening and he stopped them, making sure the fight was only one-to-one. This boy was Ben Helfgott, now Chairman of the '45 Aid Society, and Harry has known him ever since. (Ben's family had lived in Piotrków before the war but had been forced to leave their home also and go into the Ghetto.)

There was a patch of green in the Ghetto, and Harry was on it one day when a Polish boy suddenly attacked him. The Pole had a knife and sprang at Harry, trying to stab him in the face. It is unclear quite what happened next or how Harry managed to get out of this, but his quick reactions averted catastrophe. Somehow it was the attacker who was hit in the face, with a stone. Harry came away with a small knife wound on his right hand, the scar from which is still visible.

A week or two later, Harry was involved in another fight. A boy had come and told him that his brother Jona was fighting with a youth from a gang of 'no-goods' who were trying to steal his watch. When Harry got there the pair were still at it, and Jona did not look too good. Harry hit the 'no-good' on the head and knocked him down. This was doubly bad for the ruffian, as he had now lost face with his gang as well as finding himself on the ground.

Jossel and Ruchel set about making a new home and making a go of it. Jossel worked mainly on suits, turning old suits inside out and re-stitching them 'as good as new'. Harry would help him unpick the suits, using a razor blade with which to cut the old stitches. He also helped his resourceful mother in the fruit shop she had opened. This rented shop was not far away, situated just across a canal, next to the canal bridge, along the Yiddish Gas. Ruchel had reasoned that if food was your work, then there was less chance of starvation, and they managed, but the food contained little variety. The Polish farmers came into the Ghetto with fruit, mostly apples and pears, and occasional vegetables, which Ruchel bought to sell in the shop. Harry soon got hold of a piece of wood with a nail sticking out of it to stop thieves! Wallop! Fellow Ghetto dwellers should steal from the Poles, not us, he thought crossly. He used this tool with great effect to jab at potatoes or anything else he could find coming into the Ghetto on carts. Food was becoming more and more central in all their lives.

Jossel was always thinking of ways to help his family, and he began to trade in second-hand clothing. People needed money and sold their clothes for food and other necessities. People also needed clothes. Jossel would be approached if a garment was required, and he always tried to fix his customers up. Once, when he was given money by his father to go and buy a particular dress, Harry thought that he too would help the family. He offered less money for the dress than had been agreed, and the vendors refused to sell. Feeling he was in a sticky situation, and that neither the people he was with nor his family would be pleased, Harry reasoned that the best thing he could do was to leave. He could hardly say that his father had indeed given him the correct money and that it had been his own idea to reduce it! He gave all the money back to his father and said nothing. Later on, the owners of the dress turned up and said they would sell it to Jossel for the lower price, obviously thinking that it had been Jossel who had reduced his offer.

Jossel recognized his son's input and after the people had left he said, 'Now we have a businessman in the family!'

Jossel also allowed garments out on approval and always worked hard at finding the right garment for the right person.

Jossel and Ruchel did all they possibly could for their family, and the three children did what they could also. Sometimes Harry took a wooden tray of sweets out to sell. The tray was held up by a string round his neck, and the sweets were sold individually. This form of 'Ghetto vending' has been realistically portrayed in the Roman Polanski film 'The Pianist'. But life in the Ghetto got harder and darker, and every day there were shootings, beatings and killings, as well as constant abuse from incoming Germans or from Ukrainians working for the Nazis. There were also constant raids in which young men were rounded up for working parties. One day Harry watched a group of *Hitlerjugend* (Hitler Youth) marching past next to the Ghetto boundary. The leader yelled foul abuse at him, and Harry picked up a stone and hurled it. The stone hit the abuser, and Harry ran off quickly. After the Ghetto was closed, Jona and Harry continued to sneak out, pretending to be non-Jews, and would come back with coal, food and other things in exchange for tailoring work Jossel had done. This was very dangerous. If a person was caught outside the Ghetto they would be shot.

Schooling was forbidden, but little Rhuda-Pawa was sent 'on the quiet' to a hidden school which happened to be in the building where Ben Helfgott's family were now living. Harry was sent to a relative in order to continue his religious education, and Jona came with him. They would go there several times a week. Harry remembers being groomed to become a Torah reader, which involved not simply reading the Hebrew, but using particular inflections as well. This way of reciting prayers is known as *davening* and involves the upper body rocking up and down so that all senses are used in prayer. *Davening* was a hidden affair in the Ghetto as it was strictly forbidden, but at some stage Harry recalls having his Bar Mitzvah, certainly brought forward because of circumstances, as he cannot have been thirteen when it took place. The service was held on the second floor of the building next door to where they were living. Jossel had gathered a few people together, and they 'did it', for it only required a *minyan* (quorum of ten men) to be present. Jossel never hit Harry again after his Bar Mitzvah.

'You are a man now', he said.

The buildings in that part of Piotrków had outside landings with doors leading off them into rooms. Harry remembers a toddler falling from the second floor of the building he had his Bar Mitzvah in. The child fell into the yard beneath and not only survived but was barely hurt at all.

The family's one room served them for everything; cooking, sleeping, and working on clothes. There was a pump nearby for water, and Harry thinks they had managed to bring their *ballio* with them. This was a wide but shallow wooden barrel made for washing both clothes and people. Sanitation was very basic. A house not far away had been turned into a communal latrine. The ground floor was sealed, and people went upstairs, making use of holes cut into the floor. When one latrine became full, another house was taken for a similar purpose. At the end of 1941 there was a typhus epidemic and both Jossel and Ruchel were infected, but in spite of the cramped living conditions, none of the children caught it. Ruchel's hair fell out, but it grew back curly and thicker than ever. Jossel's brother, the handsome Saul, died of typhus at this time. The linseed press below their room was home to a great many rats who fed on the discarded linseed husks. Harry and others would throw stones at them, but the quantity of husks kept the rats in fodder, a fact which helped the people living there as the rats didn't bother to go upstairs. The general conditions in the Ghetto were, however, ripe for disease.

Soon there was talk of being moved again, and then the community leaders were told that if someone in a family worked for the Germans, that family would be able to stay put. Restrictions grew tighter and tighter. Jossel acted. He obtained a work card and place for Jona at the Hortensia Glass Works, a factory that made bottles, ranging from three-litre containers and ordinary bottles down to medicine bottles and handmade drinking glasses. Jona worked from early in the day and therefore did not accompany Harry to any further religious education. Eighteen months later, they were told that two people needed to work in order to avoid deportation. Jossel then got himself a job in the Karo Glass Works. In September 1942 the Gestapo began to be even more active, and rumours of deportation increased. On 13 October 1942 Jossel acted again, this time obtaining a work card for his youngest son, although he was still only twelve. This deed saved Harry's life. That very night of 13 October, orders were given out concerning the next day.

* * *

During the night of 13 October 1942, the SS, together with the Ukrainian militia, under the command of SS-Hauptsturmfuher Willy

Blum, surrounded the Piotrków Ghetto. At 2.00 am on 14 October 1942 the *'Aktion'* began, commanded by SS-Sturmbannfuher Feucht. District by district, every Jew in the Piotrków Ghetto was told to go to the main square, the Platz Trybunalski, or as the Germans called it, the Umschlagplatz, which simply means 'collecting point'. This was in order to be organized for resettlement. There was an absolute requirement that every family member attend, regardless of age or health, as everyone would be moving on, and every house was searched. One thousand sick and elderly Jews were shot on the spot before they reached the square, and the square was full of soldiers, with the SS acting as guards to prevent anyone from leaving it. A large table had been set up, behind which sat several soldiers who checked everyone's papers. Those classed as 'workers', with work papers, were separated from all the others. Thus it was that Ruchel and Rhuda-Pawa found themselves in the largest group on one side, while Jossel, Jona and Harry were on the other. Jossel, feeling that Harry was still too young to be parted from his mother, told him to go across and be with her and Rhuda-Pawa. The soldier who had checked Harry's papers got up and pushed him back over to join his father and brother, hitting Jossel for sending his son to the wrong place.

That same day, and during the next few days, every Jew of whatever age who was without work papers was taken to the station, where they were forced to board trains made up of cattle trucks. These trucks were filled to bursting point with the Ghetto's men and women, children and babies, and they were then sealed from the outside. In that October week 22,000 people were compelled to press themselves into these trains, which carried them straight to the Treblinka Death Camp, where they were all gassed upon arrival. Ruchel was thirty-eight. Rhuda-Pawa was nine.

The fact that Jossel had wanted Harry to stay with his mother is absolute proof that the family knew nothing about this. The truth of the

Final Solution and extermination had not yet filtered through, and the Nazi deception reigned. Not one of Jossel's brothers had obtained work papers. They and their families were all selected for the trains and went to Treblinka, as did almost everyone from the Gotesman families (See family trees at the beginning of the book).

Those Jews who had the appropriate work papers were taken back to work in the glass factories, which were within walking distance. Arriving first at the Hortensia Glass Works, the SS guard checked the Hortensia list, weeding out those whose names were not on it. Harry's name was not there, as Jossel had only got him the papers the day before. Five other boys of similar age were not on the list either and they were all asked to step forward. Jossel saw what happened but was forced to march on as he worked in the Karo factory, which was a little further off. Jossel believed that Harry would now be parted from him, and Harry can still see the look of trauma on his father's face as he was made to walk away.

The Managing Director at Hortensia was a *Volksdeutscher*, a person of ethnic German origin living in Poland, and he knew what fate awaited those not on the list. He also knew that Harry was Jona's brother, and Jona had worked for him for about eighteen months.

Having some humanity, he said to the SS man, 'Let me go in and check the books.'

This was a ruse. He came back and picked out Harry and another boy whose father worked there, saying that both of them did in fact, work for him. He lied and saved their lives. This was the second time in one day that Harry's life had been saved, and he knows that he owes this to his father, who acted to get Jona work and then to get Harry's work papers, quite literally just in time. The other four boys not on the list were taken to the trains.

Workers for Hortensia having been sorted out, the SS went away, pro tem. Members of the Polish Fire Brigade had been given an additional job, as guards in the factory, but these men were unarmed and altogether a different kettle of fish from the SS. The two brothers paid one of them to go over to the Karo works in order to relieve their father's agony. He was to tell Jossel that Harry was all right, and that his sons were still together. Jona and now Harry were both glass factory workers.

After work, everyone from both the Karo and Hortensia factories was marched back to the Ghetto under guard. There they were housed in strictest isolation, as the Ghetto was being liquidated and anyone still remaining there in hiding was being hunted down. That evening, Jossel and his sons were together again. For the first time in their lives they were presented with non-kosher food, and Jossel refused to eat it.

Jona and Harry both said, 'If you are not going to eat, we will not eat either.'

After that, Jossel ate anything, but this was just another way in which so much was taken from them that day.

Work in the Hortensia glass factory began for Harry on the bottom rung with the most basic menial labour. This involved the task of carrying newly made items from the machines to a conveyor belt which took the hot glass through a cooling process. In order to do this job without getting burnt they had a special grabber with which to pick up the fiery forms. Back and forth they went for the eight hours of the shift. There were three shifts per day. The factory only shut down on Sundays, when work ceased. The shift times were from 6.00 am to 2.00 pm and 2.00 pm until 10.00 pm. The night shift was from 10.00 pm until 6.00 am, and Harry hated this shift. They worked a week on one shift and then changed to another, doing each shift in turn. Polish workers still ran the factory and they had a canteen there and proper meal breaks. There was no food for any Jew during a work shift. Water they did have, and it was freely available as it was a necessity in the intense heat. The Jewish workers received soup and bread once a day, either back in the Ghetto or later on, when they were moved out of the Ghetto, in the camp. Their work was very hard and very hot. It was a man's work and they were children no longer (Plates 12 and 13).

On the journeys to and from the Ghetto they were guarded by soldiers under the SS. One morning, as they were on the way to work, a friend's brother was shot for not 'marching properly'.

Fairly soon after Harry had started in Hortensia there was a day when Jossel told him not to go to work. He had learned that the SS were on the prowl, 'cleaning up' anyone left in the Ghetto, finding those in hiding but also snatching youngsters away whilst they were en route to or from the factories. Jossel hid Harry in a *shennik*, one of the straw-filled sack mattresses that they slept on. Another day, when Jona and Harry were on the night shift, a boy called Krulik Wilder who was on their shift did not leave with them at the end of it but stayed behind in the factory, waiting for his father's shift to finish. On the way back to the Ghetto from this shift, which was managed by a *Volksdeutcher* called Edelmann, the SS seized all twenty-five young ones as they walked and took them to join five hundred other Jews being held in the Piotrków Great Synagogue. These were men, women and children who had managed to avoid the earlier selections and had been in hiding in the Ghetto. The manager of Jona's, Harry's and Krulik's shift was called Michelfreid, and Krulik was rather a pet of his. Hearing what had happened and that Krulik had been taken away with the boys from the Edelmann shift, he was upset and wanted to save his favourite. Michelfreid put up a fight with the SS, saying that he could not manage without the boys and that they were essential for his work. He knew better than to single one boy out, as this would have been both suspicious and useless and would have compromised his own safety also. He got all twenty-five boys out! Their lives were saved that day because of Krulik. (Krulik and two other boys rescued that day, Gary Winogrodski and Harry Spiro, survived the war. They became members of the '45 Aid Society, 'The Boys', and our close friends.) The five hundred remaining in the synagogue were led out to the nearby Raków Forest and made to dig their own graves. They were all shot. This massacre took place on 20 December 1942.

Things settled down a bit after this, and Harry's initiative was activated. Food, mostly potatoes, was delivered to the factory for the Polish canteen. Jewish boys were often kept on, especially after the shift which ended at 2.00 pm, in order to help take barrowloads of potatoes into the storeroom. The odd potato would be pinched, and it was easy to cook them by the side of the glass ovens. But Harry considered the 'odd potato' was insufficient for everyone and taking them this way was time-consuming. One day, when he was called upon to assist with a delivery, he went on walking with his full barrow, passing the storeroom and going into the workplace. The entire load was then tipped into a cupboard!

Lunch breaks were a difficult half hour for the Jewish workers. They were pressed into working harder than the Poles and yet had to hang around hungry when the others went to eat. During one lunch break Harry noticed that Michelfreid, who lived on the premises, had some nice apples in his garden. He climbed over the wall and stole some. Michelfreid spotted him, but Harry noticed and ran off quickly. Once back at work after the break, Michelfreid called him over. Harry knew what was coming.

Michelfreid gave him a few thumps and said, 'If you wanted apples why didn't you ask?'

Harry replied that he was sorry and was asking now.

'You can't have any,' said Michelfreid.

After the war the Poles took revenge on anything German, and Michelfreid was in a group that was executed. They were tied to cars and pulled along until they were dead.

As time went on, Harry moved up the working ladder. He wanted to do well and show the managing director who had saved him initially that he had been right to do so. By the end of his time in Hortensia Harry was doing one of the top skilled jobs, pouring molten glass into a mould. The moulds were usually for making bottles, but the factory made some large glass containers as well. The wish to do well was reinforced from time to time when the SS appeared and demanded that a number of Jews be handed over to them. When this happened, the shift would be ordered to line up and the managing director would be forced to pick out the requisite number of people, walking down the line and pointing at one and then another. He would wink at Harry as he went by as if to say, 'I didn't save your life once only to let it go now.'

Once the 'liquidation' of the Piotrków Ghetto was complete a camp was constructed closer to the glass factories. The workers from both the Hortensia and Karo factories were moved out of the Ghetto and into the new camp to live. This camp made use of an old building several storeys high as well as some new wooden huts. Jossel and his sons were housed in the old building and shared a small room with three others. On either side of this room were wooden bunks, three tiers high. Each worker was expected to turn up for his shift, but there was not a roll call every day. They were sometimes checked, however, and if anyone was missing, one of the guards went to the camp to find the reason. This would frequently end with severe beatings and broken bones for the culprits. There were several occasions when Jona was not well enough to work and he didn't go. Each time Jona stayed behind, Harry put on a different voice if there was a roll call and answered for him. Amazingly, he got away with it, but he took a not inconsiderable risk on behalf of his brother, as both of them would have been beaten up if discovered. The brothers were there for each other, a fact which outweighed all risks.

Jossel held a highly skilled job in the Karo factory. Before the war he had done some work as a glazier, including with his brothers Lazer and Saul on the glass roof of the Tuszyn sanatorium. The Karo works needed someone with the ability to repair the factory windows, a person who was able to measure and cut the glass to size, as well install it. For this repair work Jossel used the pieces of broken glass left from accidents that had occurred when sheet glass was being cut, and he obtained this job due to having a diploma as a glazier. He had two other diplomas as well, one as a furrier and the other as a tailor.

The two glass factories of Karo and Hortensia had been going for many years prior to the war and were filled with their own Polish workforce. The Jewish workers were extras, stepping up the pace of production. Some Polish workers would pick on the Jewish lads, attacking them both verbally and physically. Boys who wore the very obviously 'Jewish dress' of a long black coat and whose hair sported *payot* (side curls) were especially chosen for abuse. These Hasidic boys were useless at fighting and defending themselves, and Harry and others had to do it for them. Sixty years after the war, one of these boys named Gleiwitzer who had needed assistance then saw Krulik Wilder and asked him about Harry saying, 'Is he still fighting?'

Not all the Polish workers were distant or unkind. The master in charge of the machine where Jona and Harry worked was very nice and friendly. His name was Ruszyn and he was fair-haired and good-looking. Ruszyn became a friend from the first moment Jona started working at Hortensia, which was well before the Piotrków Ghetto was liquidated, and he would come into the Ghetto and visit the whole family. Jossel made him a suit then, and Ruszyn continued to be a loyal friend all through. An opposite attitude was taken by an older boy, a Pole, who was always picking on the Jewish lads. In the end Harry could stand it no longer and they got into a punch-up. They were fighting close to the conveyor belt which took the finished bottles off for cooling, and Harry pushed the brute's face near the belt, singing all his facial hair. He ended up with no eyebrows at all, but after this he was less of a problem.

One evening after work, a man came into their room in the camp. He was angry with Jossel over something and actually threw a pot or some such at him. It did not hurt Jossel very much, but it hit him, and that was enough for Harry, who jumped on the man from the top bunk where he had been watching what was going on. The force of this jump knocked the man to the ground, even though Harry was only twelve or thirteen years old. Harry's knees were on the man's chest, and Jossel had to pull him off, for he was not going to let anyone treat his father in that manner and get away with it. The man who caused this dispute later got into a fight with a Pole at work and was thrown out of the Hortensia factory. This would have meant almost certain death for him at the time.

As Jona and Harry were given increasingly skilled jobs they were moved away from Ruszyn's machine. The Polish workers were on piecework, so the more they did the more they got paid. All pay for Jewish workers had ceased shortly after Harry started. Once the Ghetto was liquidated completely, all Jews became slave labourers (Plate 14). When the brothers were moved to a new machine, the Polish worker there kept pressing them to do more and more as this increased his wages. Both Jona and Harry complained, 'Why should we do it?' they said. 'We don't get paid.'

In the end they came to an agreement whereby the Pole brought in two large loaves of bread for them each week. This provided extra food for Jossel as well, and the boys were glad to have helped. They knew their father was doing all he possibly could to get hold of more food and after work, and on Sundays Jossel was continuing to mend clothes for people in the camp. He did this work for money, since it was always possible to give money to a Pole who would shop outside and bring food and other things into the camp.

Once the shifts had ended, and after any odd jobs were completed such as the shifting of potatoes and the unloading of coal for the furnaces, the Jewish workers were allowed back to the camp, where they were left to their own devices. Harry and some other boys managed to get a few books together and formed a library group. Harry would also help his father in mending clothes and he sought out any job going that brought them in more food. He was given a whole loaf of bread once for cleaning someone's floor. The great recreation they had was football. There was an area of grass in the camp which made a good pitch, and the Jews would play matches there against the Polish Fire Brigade guards. Youth and energy were still strong and Harry once ran round this football pitch fifty times!

The war began to hot up and go less well for the Germans, but their persecution of the Jews continued unremittingly. Stories concerning where this ended were now coming out. In 1943 they learned the unspeakable fate of those on the Piotrków trains. The appalling truth of what had happened to Ruchel and Rhuda-Pawa and nearly all their huge family in Treblinka had filtered through. At the time the impact of this was not as great as it became after the war. Harry could not dwell on the terrible fate of his beloved mother and sister. By then they all expected that it would be theirs too, but in spite of this sense of doom, all energy was used in a bid for day-to-day survival.

It was in the autumn of 1944 that the SS came into both glass factories and ordered all Jewish workers to cease work and return to the camp. Everyone was told to gather up their belongings and board the trains made up of cattle trucks. Fear was everywhere, and hardened as he had become by now, Harry felt it all around him as a force, a palpable force that was almost something to reach out and touch. For where the trains went was now known by all.

Their train took them to Częstochowianka a Jewish slave-labour camp. Steel was made in the camp and German tanks were repaired. Large shells were armed and stored there too. Częstochowianka, named after the nearby town of Częstochowa, revealed itself at once as a very different animal from the camp they had left. On arrival everyone was put into huts. It was no longer six to a room. These huts contained hundreds of people each. Jossel and his sons were given one bunk for the three of them. Everything was filthy dirty and infested with bugs and lice. There had been bedbugs at the glass factory camp, but they had managed to remain fairly clean. From this moment on until the end of the war, dirt and lice were upon them to the extent that they were able to put their hands inside their jackets and pull out handfuls of them. It was here in Częstochowianka that their captors took away their names. They were each given a number and from now on they were known only by these. Jossel's number was 102669. Jona's was 102649 and Harry's was 102647.

In the glass factories they had always been hungry, but it had been possible to obtain some extra food. In Częstochowianka extra food was completely unavailable. Their daily ration comprised a revolting soup of water and potato flakes, plus a slice of dark bread. This was served inside the huts in the evening. In the mornings a fellow prisoner, someone who had been in the camp for a long time and had been put in charge of other 'heflings' (how Harry pronounced the German word *Häftling*, a word used mainly for Jewish prisoners) and who was known as a *Kapo* (man in charge), together with some helpers, came to fetch everyone out for work. This work was any menial task at all and included having to carry the live shells used in tanks from where they were completed to the storerooms. Everyone's health deteriorated, and they suffered painfully from hunger which kept them awake and gnawed without reprieve. The three would rub each other to keep warm and attempt to wash each other in a bid to keep clean, but the filth was uncontrollable. It may have been here (Harry cannot remember in which camp this happened) that he was given the job of loading dead bodies onto lorry after lorry. When there was a break whilst waiting for the next lorry to arrive, they sat down. There were no seats, and they sat on the stiff corpses.

They had been in Częstochowianka a few weeks when the Germans, who were being forced to retreat by the advancing Russians, liquidated the camp. Hut by hut, everyone was assembled, but then some numbers were called out from the main group. They were told that these numbers were people who would be sent elsewhere, and both Jona's and Harry's numbers were called, but not Jossel's. Not wanting to be parted from his sons, Jossel stepped forward and volunteered to go with them. If he had not done this he might have lived, as the real hardship was yet to come, and those few who remained in Częstochowianka were liberated much earlier. Each person was given a small loaf of bread and made to board a train of cattle trucks, which were once again closed from the outside. One hundred and twenty people were pushed into each truck. There was no water at all. There was no sanitation, no room to move, no light and very little air. At one point the train stopped in a station. Harry happened to be next to the truck wall and, looking through a chink, he saw that they were in Vienna. The train took three days to arrive at Buchenwald

Concentration Camp, where they had to wait again before the doors were opened. Several people did not survive this journey.

Whilst in the train Harry met someone who had escaped from an extermination camp. He told Harry all about it and what happened there: how you were told to take your clothes off, then you were shaved all over and sent to the showers; only the showers were not showers, they were gas chambers that killed you. In the circumstances, this was the last thing Harry wanted to hear, and he felt a sense of doom on entering Buchenwald. However, when he was reunited with Jossel and Jona he never breathed a word and carried this horror alone through all that ensued.

What occurred on arrival in Buchenwald seemed to signify to Harry that it was indeed the end. They were taken into a large building and made to undress completely. They had to leave their clothes and shoes in a particular place and were then shouted at to 'Go down there!' They were forced underground, down some stairs. This felt very bad indeed. Shaving came next. Other inmates shaved them, and every hair on their bodies was painfully and roughly removed, leaving their skin acutely sore. Disinfectant was then sprayed all over them. Next, they were made to enter a disinfectant bath, standing in the liquid up to their necks. Being so raw from the shaving, this caused them terrible pain, and Harry thought that this must be it, this must be the method used to kill you in this camp.

An eternity passed. Real showers followed, and from there they progressed to yet another place, where they were given some clothes comprising a jacket, a pair of trousers and some shoes. No undergarments were given, and the jacket and trousers were worn next to the skin. All these clothes were taken from the piles they had recently taken off, but they did not get their own clothes back and so they didn't fit. Oddly, Jossel was given a coat that he recognized as belonging to someone he knew. In the Ghetto a man named Schotland had come to Jossel.

'You are the tailor' he said. 'Could you sew my dollars into my coat?'

Jossel did this for him. Dollars were very good to have, and Jossel understood. Later, when still in the Ghetto, Schotland became worried. He became obsessed with the idea that Jossel knew where his money was hidden and he took it out of his coat and put it into his shoes. This was a mistake. Jossel would have given him the money from his coat, whereas in Buchenwald Schotland never saw his shoes again.

Once the clothes had been put on it was outside again into the freezing air. They had suffered the days of nightmare on the train, and the ordeal of the disinfectant. Now, with totally inadequate apparel, they were made to endure standing in the open for more than seven hours, until the entire trainload had been processed. Everyone was given a category, and Harry was classed as not only Jewish, but a political prisoner as well!

Block 66 was a transit block and very large, containing hundreds of people. Jossel, Jona and Harry ended up in this block, together with others from their train. Not long after they had all come inside they were visited by three Jewish inmates who were camp veterans. These three were communists and had probably been imprisoned before the war. One of them had red hair and was commonly known as Ginger. He asked if there was anyone amongst them who had been cruel or who was an informer 'or anything'. Ginger told them to point such people out.

One boy spoke up saying, 'Because of this man here, my father was killed.'

The three veterans invited the boy to deliver the first punch. This happened to one or two people, who were then taken out of the block and never seen again.

As in Częstohwianka, foul-smelling soup and a slice of bread were served out once a day, but in Buchenwald the problem of hunger became all-consuming and was exacerbated by idleness. They had no work to help take their mind off it. There was too much time to think, and the longing for food was agony. As they had no idea of how long they were to remain there, time assumed endless proportions. Once or twice, no more, they were taken out of the block and sent to work on the local railway. Beside the railway track was a hut used by the *Kapo*. This hut was warm inside, and the *Kapo* stayed in it while the others were working in the freezing cold. The *Kapo* chose Harry and took him into the hut, giving him food and keeping him there in the warm. Harry thought this was wonderful! The next day, they were sent to work in the same place, but Jossel told his son that he was not to go to the hut any more. Harry was incredulous and argued his case with vigour.

'Never mind why not,' said Jossel. 'You're not going.'

Harry then accepted what his father said, totally and at once. The three were of one mind, and Jossel was given absolute authority. What Jossel said, went. They depended on each other for life itself. Later, Harry found out about homosexuality and realized what the *Kapo* had had in mind. He was fourteen when this happened, and still naïve.

Keeping going was now a daily battle, and everything was done to try and stay alive. A special way of walking, known throughout all the Concentration Camps as 'the camp walk' was first adopted by Jossel and his sons in Buchenwald. This was a kind of stooping glide, perfected in order to use the minimum amount of energy. Harry remembers batches of new people coming into the camp from Hungary and how amazed these people were at the sight of all the creeping skeletons. The Hungarians came into this hell straight from their homes; only days before, 'they had been eating chicken soup'. They had had no years of privation to toughen them up as had the Jews from Poland. By the end of two weeks the 'creeping skeletons' were still creeping, but the 'fat' Hungarians were in a most pitiful state.

The *Kapo* of Block 66 was a German criminal. One day, hunger got the better of Harry and he approached this man, which was a highly dangerous thing to do.

'I'm hungry,' said Harry.

'Didn't you get a soup?' said the *Kapo*.

'Yes', said Harry, 'but I'm still hungry.'

Astonishingly, the *Kapo* told those serving to give Harry another soup. Hungry as he was, he shared it with his father and brother. It was in Buchenwald that Harry noticed that the people serving out the soup were not quite so hungry. Any soup that was left over, they got. This was an important observation and would be made use of later.

There was a Children's Block in Buchenwald, and they found out that little Isaac Fuks was in it, although they were not able to see him. Isaac was the son of Jossel's first cousin, the legendary, strong Joino, and grandson of the Isaac from the dairy in Tuszyn. This Isaac, was eight years younger than Harry, making him about six years old when he was in Buchenwald, and child though he was, he was also classed as a political prisoner! In Buchenwald Jossel and his sons discovered, one way or another, that Isaac's father Joino had been in Buchenwald also but had been sent on to the slave labour camp at Schlieben in Germany, leaving little Isaac behind. In Schlieben, volunteers were asked for to return to Buchenwald, and Joino put himself forward, wanting to rejoin his son. This was another deception. All this group were shot on the way. Jossel, Jona and Harry learned about this from others who had been in Schlieben, but not having seen either Joino or his son Isaac since the Piotrków Ghetto, they did not find out how it was that little Isaac especially had avoided the Treblinka trains.

The seemingly endless time in Buchenwald was to finish abruptly after about three weeks, but of course they had had no knowledge of if, or when, they were to leave. Suddenly were made to board another cattle train, but this journey was quite a short one, taking them to the vast working complex of Mittelbau-Dora. On arrival here, all their clothes were exchanged for the trademark striped pyjamas, the thin blue and white striped jacket, trousers and cap that are such a symbol of the Camps. Buchenwald was the Concentration Camp that supplied slave labour for Mittelbau-Dora, which was thus both a camp and a work place, situated in Lower Saxony, Germany. Hidden inside the mountain there, the V1 flying bombs and later the V2 rockets were made that would cause a new wave of terror in Britain. It was the work of the slave labourers in Dora to hew out the stone of the mountain, going deep inside, to enlarge the space for rocket production. This was the toughest of manual labour and for starving workers almost impossible. Hundreds of thousands died, and Harry saw people committing suicide on the electric fences in preference to the indescribable suffering of this work.

The camp living quarters at Dora were very efficiently run, and the soup thicker than in Buchenwald. The three were placed in this camp at first, and Harry noticed the German guards themselves were serving the soup. Making use of his Buchenwald observation, that those who served the food were a little less hungry, Harry used his initiative. He went up to the guards who were serving and addressed them obsequiously.

'This is not a job for *you* to have to do!! This is not a job for soldiers!! I would be happy to do this for you.'

The soldiers agreed, telling him to find two others to help him. In fact, the guards were quite pleased not to have to do this job, and it meant that Harry and the other two had any leftovers. Harry shared his leftovers with Jossel and Jona, and soon with someone else. The new person's brother had recently died after a bullet lodged in his back had caused the wound to fester. This boy that they took into their group was quite alone. His nickname was Katchmarik. They shared their food with him and saved his life. Nobody survived who was on their own. Katchmarik lived into old age, and features in Harry's story after the war.

Another encounter over the soup in Dora was to have unforeseen but hugely significant consequences. A Russian prisoner in line for his soup had eaten quickly and come up again for a second helping. The guards, who were now not serving but who were watching the proceedings, accused this Russian of having come round twice. Harry spoke up for him, saying he had not come round again and pointing out that every Russian looked alike. This amused the guards, and they let the Russian go. Harry had saved him from a bad beating, after which broken bones and open wounds frequently meant death as well as pain and misery. The Russian became very friendly after this and he never forgot what had been done for him.

From the camp at Dora it was only a short walk to the workplace in the mountain where they had to clear away the heavy stone and put it into trolleys which were on a small railway track to facilitate its removal. Dora had another section where the V1 and V2 rockets were filled with explosives. This section was cordoned off and was a forbidden area, but it was warm. Harry once crept into it to warm up, but he was spotted and slapped about the face.

'*Schweinhund*'! shouted the guard, making him return to the other side.

Harry got off lightly and owes this to his father who taught his sons an important lesson: 'Never cover your face and you may get away with slaps. If you cover your face, you will be beaten with a rifle butt.'

A band played at the entrance to and exit from work. Several people, often corpses already, eight or so at a time, were also displayed there, hanging from a gibbet. Death from one cause or another was all around. Jossel, Jona and Harry all worked together at first, but Harry only did the backbreaking work in the stone quarry for a short time. This was because a German Gypsy, who had some standing as a long-term prisoner, approached the Germans.

'Have you lost all humanity?' he said. 'How could you expect children to do this work? They can't do it!'

He was able to take Harry and some other young ones out of the quarry and into work in the SS kitchens, peeling potatoes. This was comparative *heaven* as a job and had life-saving perks. For example, the boys were allowed to take one pot of soup out of the kitchen at the end of the day. Only soup was permitted to leave the premises, no potatoes. Harry took his pot for his father and brother. Sometimes as they left the kitchens a guard would check their pots for any forbidden content. Harry knew that it was vital to get some extra hot food for Jossel and Jona and he was determined to get some potatoes to them as well. He managed to get hold of a spoon that was too short to reach to the bottom of his soup pot, thus not reaching the potatoes he had hidden there. This spoon safeguarded both the potatoes and himself should his soup be checked!

Being in the kitchen meant food, and food meant life. The youngsters peeled the potatoes with as much flesh left on the peelings as possible. Every scrap of peel was saved, cooked, and either eaten at work or taken out for others in the soup pot. One day when an SS guard came to inspect them, he demanded that they peel the potatoes more thinly. From now on they complied when the SS were present. When alone again, they went back to the thick peelings. This extra food was the difference between life and death. (Such is the strength of Harry's association with potato peelings that he will not eat them now, carefully removing the thinnest scrap of peel from the newest cooked potato.) No one could have survived without it, but it was not an easy matter to get hold of additional food in Dora. There were a few hundred other people who wanted it as well, and these begged and beseeched Harry to give them some. He had to say no to them all. He only had enough for Jossel and Jona.

The Gypsy who had made the life-saving kitchen work possible was later caught in a compromising situation with a boy. They were hanged at the same time, and everyone was brought out and forced to watch.

There were some German women working in the SS kitchens who felt sorry for the boys, seeing the state of them, and they began to bring in a little food for the young ones. But this did not last long. The SS decided that it was not suitable for German women to be associating with Jewish boys, so they put the eighteen boys into a separate hut for their potato peeling. It was so cold that there had to be a stove in this hut to prevent the potatoes from freezing and becoming impossible to peel. A stove meant cooking, and pots of potatoes were on the boil. A lookout was always on watch, and one day he warned that an SS man was coming. They rushed to clear away the evidence, but two pots remained and were seen. The boys knew that they would be thrown out of the kitchen, which was the lifeline for them and their dependants. To be thrown out would be as bad as being shot.

One of the boys said to Harry, 'You are the talker, go and talk to him.'

It was unheard of to be able to talk to the SS, but Harry went out after the man.

'*Ein moment bitte, Herr General.* We are very very hungry as we have been given no bread in the camp. We don't *usually* do this. Please do not tell on us.'

Somehow, Harry got to him.

'Don't let the Governor catch you,' was all the SS man said.

They had got away with it, and he did not report them. The eighteen boys were able to continue in the kitchen, and this certainly contributed to the survival of Harry and Jona, Josh Segal and his brother, David

Hirschfeld, his brother Moniac and the others. Harry remembers David and Moniac shaving off their few whiskers when in the potato hut, and some of the older boys shaved every day. It was only due to their youth that they were able to do this job in the first place, and it meant literally everything to them to be able to keep it.

At the end of one day's work they were unexpectedly not marched back to the camp at Dora, but taken by train to the notorious camp at Nordhausen. This was in order to make room for a new influx of prisoners, since Dora was bursting at the seams. In Nordhausen, enormous concrete industrial warehouses were used as a camp for thousands of people. Wire cages were built inside containing bunks. There was no heating or sanitation in the buildings, which had been used originally for the finishing and storage of new cars. The wired areas were like animal cages. At the time of food distribution they were locked, ensuring nobody was able to come round for more. Prisoners were fed a cage at a time. After the food had finished, the cages were unlocked, to enable those who could still make it to stagger across the vast area to the back of the buildings and the latrines. Weakness and illness frequently made this journey impossible. Life expectancy in Nordhausen was three weeks.

Jossel, Jona and Harry were in Nordhausen in midwinter, the winter of 1944/45. It was freezing cold, with bitter winds, snow and ice. In Dora, the camp had been close to the workplace so time for sleeping was longer. Nordhausen was a train ride away, and this added to the misery. Prisoners were roused at 4.30 am and were made to stand outside and be counted. This procedure was called *Appel*. If the count was correct they were able to move off; if not, they remained standing until after a number of re-counts the SS 'had' to let them go to work. They were then marched to the station. The train bound for Dora usually left on time, work being a priority. In the evening, however, at seven or eight o'clock, when work was finished for the day, returning the prisoners back to Nordhausen no longer took priority. There were frequent delays, and the train was often shunted into a siding to wait. In Nordhausen food was never given before 10.00 pm, and delays sometimes meant getting no food until 11.00 pm. Normally they were given a soup and a slice of bread at 10.30 pm and were able to go to bed by 12.30 am. People could not survive this for long, but worse followed. When Jossel and his sons first arrived there was the usual slice of bread with the soup. Then there was just the soup. No bread. It was not uncommon to be talking to someone, and when they did not answer it was because they were dead.

Nordhausen was a killing field delivering death by starvation, overwork and torture. One method of torture Harry remembers being inflicted on them concerned the so-called 'cleaning' of prisoners. In sub-zero temperatures, cage by cage, they were ordered to undress. Totally naked, they were then forced to walk outside into the snow towards a side of the warehouse where factory equipment was located. Once there, huge industrial hoses were turned on them, and their shivering, skeletal bodies were hosed down with powerful jets of icy water. While their fellow human beings inflicted this additional torment on the prisoners, the soldiers were enjoying the fun and laughed and found it an entertainment. When the perpetrators began to be bored, and only then, were the human icicles permitted to walk back to their cages. Many of those who had gone out into the snow for the sport of their captors did not make it back, for this hideous farce was simply another way of killing. The fact that the SS forced *Kapos* and other inmates to turn these hoses of death onto their fellows while they simply stood about and enjoyed the joke is a typical example of how things were done. They made prisoners do their dirty work for them.

The kitchen in Nordhausen was on the ground floor of the same building that housed Jossel, Jona and Harry, whose cage was on the floor above. This was the only kitchen for the thousands of inmates, and it made the watery soup and the bread, until the bread was stopped for the *Häftlinge*, the Jewish slave-labour prisoners. As the only kitchen it also provided the food for all the guards, and they had meat and other nutritious things. The Russian from Dora was working in this kitchen and he happened to catch sight of Harry and told him to 'come to the kitchen at any time!' In their darkest hour here was an astonishing ray of light. Harry went to his Russian friend every morning before going off to work, and again every evening when he came back. The Russian gave him sandwiches (!), as well as extra soup and potatoes to eat on the spot. It was too dangerous to take any food out. This was a feast, and totally unheard of in Nordhausen.

The guards in this kitchen got used to seeing Harry going in there, and one day his Russian friend said, 'The guards are looking for entertainment. What can we do?'

There was an inmate who had boasted that he would be able to eat 'ten soups' in one sitting. A normal thing to say when you are starving. Harry proposed to the guards that he would go and fetch this man as a diversion for them. The guards thought it was a good idea but they said if the man did not manage to eat all ten soups he would be punished by getting a beating. Harry went to the fellow concerned, and he agreed to come, being over the moon at the thought of all that food. He started to eat the soup. The first few 'soups' went down very quickly, but at about number six he began to slow down. His stomach was not able to cope with this amount of food, and soup number eight was only partially consumed. After this he was as sick as a dog, and all the soup came back up. The guards enjoyed this immensely and laughed their heads off. Now for the punishment, they said. Harry persuaded them not to beat the fellow up by indicating that they had had their fun after all. Whilst all this was going on, both Harry and the soup-eater had missed their 'official' food. Once back on the floor above, the soup-eater approached those who were serving, saying that he had been sick in the latrines, which was why he had not been there at the proper time. Harry cannot remember if he was given a soup then or not.

In the workplace at Dora the stone was hewn from the mountain with pickaxes and then carried by hand to heave into carts to be taken away. The watery soup at night was all the sustenance the workers had. Starving and exhausted, Jossel's legs began to cause him serious problems, and he wrapped them in paper in an attempt to warm them up. But his legs began to swell up, perhaps because he had tied the paper too tightly, and one day he was unable to walk. There was a place in Nordhausen for those unable to walk and go to work. This so-called hospital and its unimaginable sufferings have been well documented. The dead and the dying were simply left alone. They lay in every kind of filth and excreta. They had no care or anything to relieve their pain. The 'sickbay' did allow rest from work, however, and some people did come out of it able to walk again. When Jossel was forced to go there, Jona and Harry were hoping and expecting that he, too, would return. But he never did, and he must have died there. Harry thinks this would have been in January 1945.

Not long after Jossel had left them, the boys were moved again. Jossel's absence 'felt terrible', but he had passed on to them a vital legacy, and the discipline that he had instilled in them helped them to survive the time ahead. All the way and in every situation he had constantly encouraged them, 'Don't give up, we'll make it, we'll get through this!' He had sustained them through all the horrors. His spirit was indomitable, his courage unwavering, and his selfless care for Jona and Harry never dimmed. Jossel had also taught his boys that however desperate they were for food, they must not eat it all at once, but learn to spread it, a bite at a time, to stay alive. When Harry had been able to bring out extra food he had always handed it to Jossel first, for his father to share out between them, giving him true respect and status. Before the war Harry had found his father difficult. By the time of his death, Jossel knew beyond all doubt that he had a son. Whatever the tensions there had once been between them, these had long since vanished. Jossel had risen up to safeguard his own. It was Jossel who had bothered to obtain the work permits for Jona and then Harry that brought them to the Hortensia Glass Factory instead of the train to Treblinka. Jossel's brothers, who had not 'bothered' to do this, all perished with their families. It was Jossel who did not give up or give in. Even in the hell of Nordhausen he went on being a tower of strength to his boys until his legs could support him no longer.

It must be realized that death was everywhere and that nobody by this stage thought they would live. They only strove to live another day, another hour, or another step, just one more, and Jossel had kept this flame of endurance alight.

Jona and Harry were moved once again, to another of Dora's camps, called Hertzung. Compared to Nordhausen, Hertzung was better, having purpose-built huts which were newer and cleaner. The brothers joined up with two other boys, Josh Segal and his brother. They were friends, sharing everything and helping each other in the bid to stay alive. The trust and understanding of one another was absolute. Hertzung was closer to Dora than Nordhausen, but still some distance away, and they were forced to march there and back, transport being deemed unnecessary. A day came when Harry's legs would not support him during the four-mile march to work, and Josh held him up, saving his life. Harry did the same thing for Josh some days later, for those who fell by the wayside were either shot or beaten to death.

On their arrival in Hertzung Harry had been detailed to work within the camp, carrying bread and food out to its working parties rather than going back to his work in Dora. This provided him with plenty of food to give to all of them, but he was only given this job on the first day. On the following day he was given a job which did not involve food. This was no good at all, and he knew that without extra food the end was a certainty for them. Taking action, Harry went to see Hertzung's notorious head *Kapo*, a German criminal who had been imprisoned for his crimes. This man was in charge of all the other *Kapos* and all the prisoners. Harry said to him that he didn't want to work in Hertzung, he wanted to go back to work in Dora 'with the men', implying that he was a man and not a boy. He wanted to go back and work in the SS kitchens, but he kept this quiet. The *Kapo* was a well-known sadist and he owned a fearful dog which he delighted in letting loose on the inmates. He threatened Harry with everything he could think of.

'Your blood will run,' he screamed, shouting abominations of all kinds.

Harry stood his ground. In the end the *Kapo* smiled, agreeing with Harry's request!

'One of these days …', smirked the *Kapo*. 'One of these days …', and he wagged his finger, calling Harry 'the camp lawyer'.

On another day when they came face to face with the SS commandant he went so far as to introduce Harry.

'See this fellow,' he said. 'He's the camp lawyer!'

Harry felt that this sadist quite liked him because he had stood up to him. This was most unusual, for obvious reasons. Harry dismisses any attempts to say that he was brave over this – 'What else was there to do?' If he had not been able to return to the Dora SS kitchens, none of them would have made it, especially his brother Jona, who was still working in the Dora stone quarry.

Whilst they were in Hertzung the Germans decided that instead of cutting slices of bread for individuals, they would simply give out a loaf for six or eight people to divide between themselves. This created a terrible problem amongst those who were starving, and having friends was crucial. Harry, Jona and their friends trusted each other with their lives and they never had fights over the bread. Jossel had taught his sons to be disciplined and never eat all the bread at once. His teaching was still adhered to, and they always saved some bread for the next day. Gangs went round at night trying to steal food. These were mostly Russian soldiers, big men. They held people down and pinched their bread.

Harry, Jona and their friends slept on the same bunks and had a system, keeping their bread on the top bunk and watching out if gangs were coming. Harry kept a lump of wood and once hit over the head a gang member who approached them, knocking him down. He was still out cold in the morning. Armed with this lump of wood, they took it in turns to guard the bread.

The war was coming closer and closer as the Russians and the Western Allies advanced. Harry had not been in Hertzung for long when the Germans decided to close the camp. Everyone was told to make ready and they were given a loaf of bread each. Between 2,500 and 3,000 of them marched to the station and boarded a cattle-truck train. The guards placed some of the KZ (*KatZet*, commonly used shorthand for *Konzentrationslager*, Concentration Camp) striped jackets on the roof of the train to try and protect themselves from being bombed, as they had to travel with the prisoners.

After they had travelled for a day or two, some British fighter-bombers were spotted when the train was in a station. These planes were the two-engine type which carried one bomb on their belly, plus machine guns. The guards unlocked the closed cattle trucks. A bomb hit the station, another bomb hit their train's engine and a third hit a passenger train standing next to them. People on the passenger train ran out into some woods, but the planes used their machine guns to mow them down, and about a hundred were killed. Only one of the prisoners was hit, in the arm. The Hertzung prisoners seized the chance to jump into the passenger train and look for food, while its passengers were in the forest. They took whatever food they found, as nothing had been given them since the initial loaf of bread. When the bombers had gone, the guards were angry and upset that a hundred people from the passenger train had been killed. They took out six prisoners and shot them, on the pretext that they had been stealing food. As their train's engine was now immobilized, the guards ordered everyone out and they began to walk. This is how their Death March began.

Not even the guards knew where to go. If they were walking one way, when they heard the guns of the approaching war, they turned off and took another direction. They marched 'any which way'. On some days they marched for fifty kilometres. When they heard guns, they stopped. When the gunfire eased off, they got up and went on. The prisoners were not given any food, except for one occasion when the guards handed out condensed milk. This caused diarrhoea – and some deaths.

In the early days of the March a guard ordered Harry to carry his rucksack for him. Harry refused, saying that he 'couldn't do it, it was hard enough to carry himself along.' After some attempts the guard gave up and left Harry alone. He realized the task was impossible.

They stopped where they could for the night. Sometimes they were lucky and found a barn in which to shelter; otherwise, they slept out in the open in fields or by the road. If they found cigarette butts on the road, they picked them up and removed the tobacco to exchange for food when they came to a village. It was winter and bitterly cold. They had a blanket each which they carried during the day. Some people found it too difficult to carry their blanket and at night would attempt to steal one from someone else. Harry and his friends wrapped themselves in their blankets like sausages and then tied themselves up with string. They stayed close together, friends safeguarding each other's blankets.

One night as they were settled in a field, they witnessed the bombing of a nearby city. The city was Dresden and this landmark event dates that stage of the March to 13, 14 or 15 February 1945.

Whenever they stopped, Harry and others would sneak out of the group to get food. In the fields it was possible to find potatoes. The farmers made mounds of potatoes and covered them in order to store them. Harry found a marrow once. They would beg for food if they passed through a village, and sometimes they were given some. In one village Harry and a friend came back with two sacks of potatoes. If they had been caught begging they would have been shot. Later on in the year, he gathered handfuls of nettles from beside the road and stuffed them under his striped jacket, next to his skin, but he never remembers being stung. Once or twice, they passed near some PoW camps, and the PoWs threw them some food over the wire fence. One of these camps was for women. The marchers were scavengers, finding bits and pieces, anything they could eat. They were never short of water, from streams and rivers, and they would start cooking potatoes, and often nettles, the moment they stopped. Some hot food was essential for life. Harry still cannot understand about the nettles. Why he was never stung remains a mystery to him.

One village they went through had a farm and a barn where the guards put them for the night. Harry and his friend Ozier, being small, were used to crawl into the farm's food store. They handed the food out to the others and then got some for themselves. They stripped this farm of all the food they could get. When they had done all this work, a huge Russian tried to take Harry and Ozier's food off them, but another Russian got hold of his thieving compatriot and gave him a good hiding.

'Let them alone!' he said. 'They got the food for you! Let them alone!'

After this helpful intervention Harry and his friends became quite friendly with this Russian, who was a bit older than them.

The Germans operated a simple system on the Death March. Anyone who was unable to walk was shot and left by the road where they fell. Jona (who had suffered terribly in the Dora stone quarry) wanted to sit down many times, but Harry talked him out of it. After some weeks Jona simply could not walk and he did sit down.

Harry said, 'If you sit down, I will have to sit with you.'

Harry and his friend Josh Segal got Jona up, and with one of them on either side, helped him to walk on. At another time, Josh Segal's brother stopped walking, and Harry helped Josh with him. As the weeks went by, there were fewer and fewer people on the march, so many had died of starvation or been shot. There came a moment when those who were left all sat down. Not long before this, following a night in a barn, the guards had taken a lorry from the farm in order to carry their stuff and generally help them. When the remaining marchers all sat down, this lorry picked up as many of them as it could carry and drove them for the rest of that day. After this, the lorry always carried some prisoners, whilst the others walked. One day, Harry was meant to go in the lorry with Jona. At the last minute, Harry went back into the barn where they had spent the night to fetch something, and when he came out, the lorry had gone; and this time it disappeared and never returned to the March. By going back into the barn Harry became separated from Jona for the first time.

The marchers went on walking. They were all in a most desperate and pitiable condition by now, but they behaved very well; they were still human and continued to help each other. Food occupied 99 per cent of their consciousness. Absolutely nothing mattered but how they could organize something to eat. Harry thought, as did they all, that *without doubt* they would end up in an extermination camp, but as it happened, a day or two after the lorry had gone for good, they came to the Concentration Camp of Theresienstadt. The date of their arrival has been discovered as being 24 April 1945. If they had not arrived here, an extermination camp would have been unnecessary. Out of the 2,500–3,000 men and boys who had begun the March, a few had gone 'somewhere' on the lorry, and there were just forty-five left who entered the camp on foot. Their guards came in with them. Some of guards had run away on the March, especially when there were fewer and fewer people to guard. The forty-five remnants from Hertzung, who had kept going, and kept going with no hope on the horizon, finally stopped walking at the beginning of the last week of April 1945. Staying together, they were housed in the fort's barracks and given some food. Harry remembers they had some bread, not very much, but it had a slither of butter on it! Butter had not been seen for years. They were also given some soup. Nothing much happened now except they were able to rest and eat some food.

Some days passed. One night they went to sleep as usual, but in the morning they looked out of the window and saw Russian tanks in the square below! They had not been aware of any fighting during the night. When they had gone to bed the Germans were there. In the morning the Germans had all vanished. They went down and found Russian soldiers, no Germans. One Russian officer talked to them in Yiddish. This was the morning of 8 May 1945.

The war was over and against all the odds, they were still alive.

Chapter 4

8 May–14 August 1945

At once, on the day of liberation, Harry and some friends left Theresienstadt and went to Litomerice, which was about two kilometres away and the nearest town to the camp. There they found deserted shops, whose owners had fled that morning. All the goods were simply left behind, and the boys took cigarettes as these were more useful than money. They found food also and took that. Harry remembers some of the older people taking jewellery and all sorts of other things, but for him and the other youngsters money had no meaning whatsoever; they were simply interested in food, and cigarettes were the currency used to get it. There was an old man in the camp who looked as if he would die at any moment, but after the liberation he revived and went out, coming back with sacks of jewellery and watches. One day, when the group were making their way to Litomerice, they came across literally thousands of German prisoners of war on the road. The Russians told everyone not to worry about the Germans; they could leave them alone as they were all going straight to Siberia. Harry went up to a very tall German PoW and stopped him.

'Take off your boots!' he demanded.

The German took his boots off 'as quiet as a lamb', and Harry kept them for years as a souvenir. This was a symbolic gesture, but it meant something very deep. At the start of the Death March Harry, as he was barefoot, had concluded negotiations to give up a piece of bread in exchange for some boots. Agreement had been reached and the deal was done, but Harry ate the bread and so got no boots. He had marched for weeks with rags tied round his feet, and in the wet, snow and mud, the rags became very heavy. Sixty years later, a wry smile can be seen on Harry's lips at the memory of those German boots given up so meekly and so soon after liberation.

Typhus and other diseases soon caused the Russians to close Theresienstadt in an attempt to contain the infection. The camp was quarantined and nobody was allowed out. Harry, however, was able to leave the camp whenever he wished, and leave 'officially'. The Russian friend who had intervened to help him and Ozier was found to be an officer, a captain, who had some authority. They had not known of his rank before, but now he was back in uniform the Russian captain had been placed in charge of an area of liberated Theresienstadt. They met again in the camp and he told Harry to ask him for anything he wanted. Others got out of the camp by 'ways and means', but Harry asked for official passes and so was free to come and go without difficulty.

Harry's leadership qualities emerged, and he was soon the leader of a gang. They organized themselves in a very fair way. For example, a boy named Denderovitch was not very good at collecting food, so his job was to do the cooking, whilst others gathered the supplies. It was vital for them to acquire more substantial food. Meagre rations were still issued in the camp, and after the Russians came there was a place where you could go and get milk and bread, but they were desperate for more sustenance. One boy in their room gathered bread, tons of it, and piled it up almost to the ceiling. If anyone so much as looked at it, they were in danger. After over five years of starvation, food was more precious than anything. The gang went not only to Litomerice but to surrounding farms, where they asked for chickens, now freely handed over to them. The chickens were brought back into the camp alive and tied to the bed legs until required. After liberation they had been allocated rooms, which they shared, but which contained proper beds. With the Germans having fled, Czechoslovak *kronas* were easy to come by, and quite soon the gang went to a restaurant in the town. Harry remembers that they each ordered two portions of potatoes and some soup.

The gang had a good line in nicking bicycles, too, and Harry nabbed a motorbike once, but it was of no use as he was unable to ride it. He also pinched a Luger.

On one foray into Litomerice they came across a German soldier. They wanted revenge, and it took six of them to chuck him into the Danube. It is staggering to recall that they were all quite glad when they saw him begin to swim out, unharmed. They were not killers.

They settled down in Theresienstadt. A week or two after liberation, some people went back to Poland to see if any family had survived. Harry asked them to look out for any of his family, and a week or two after this, Harry and Jona came across each other in a street of the camp! Great happiness indeed! Jona and those on the lorry had been liberated by Czech partisans in Linz, and he had made his way back to Poland and to Tuszyn. After all that had happened, Jona stayed only one night in Tuszyn, and this night was spent hiding in the attic of one of the family's former houses. He got out as fast as he could the following morning and said he was in fear of his life. All the family's property had been taken over, and the people in it did not want to give it back. Somehow, Jona had met some of the Death March survivors in Poland and found out that Harry was in Theresienstadt, so he went there to find him. By the time Jona arrived, Harry was well established as a leader, and his little gang was well known.

The Russians had set up a hospital for the sick, including children. After some weeks, a group of English Jews arrived and began to take care of the boys. These English Jews were from the Central British Fund, which had been created in 1933 in order to help refugees fleeing from Hitler. A doctor examined Harry and told him to eat plenty of fatty food, intimating that if he did so he would be all right. They had *all* hoped to go to Palestine and be *safe*, especially when the reception in Poland had been so bad, but the quota system in place under the British Mandate meant that Palestine was not an option. England itself was beckoning, as King George VI invited a thousand orphans from the Concentration Camps under the age of sixteen to come and make their home there. In the end, a thousand could not be found. The number that came was 723, and some of those, including Jona, were older and had lied about their age. Harry lied about his own age to assist him (Plates 15, 16 and 17).

A few of those who had gone back to Poland in search of relatives had found some and brought them back to Theresienstadt. These people had perhaps been in hiding or had posed as non-Jews. The Czechs, however, were not keen to let in more refugees and would arrest them at the border, putting them in jail inside Theresienstadt.

By chance one day, Harry spotted a cousin called Hanka, one of those who had been arrested at the Czech border. She was out walking with a female guard, and Harry called over to her to scarper, but Hanka was too afraid to do so and allowed herself to be taken back into the jail. Discovering that there were five people in the cell with Hanka that he knew, as well as two others, Harry decided to act. By this time, as a gang leader, he had some clout. He also had plenty of cigarettes, and one 'could get anything one wanted for cigarettes'. Harry got hold of a Russian soldier who was looking after the jail area and persuaded him to help in releasing Hanka and the others so that they could join the group that would be going to England. Harry gave the Russian a few hundred cigarettes and they went into the jail. The jail had two guards.

The Russian, who was armed, told the two guards to face the wall or be killed. Harry took away the guards' guns and their keys and, looking into each cell, found the right one and opened the door. He took out all eight people, including the two he did not know.

As it happened, the Czechs and Russians were working together, and the Czech authorities complained to the Russians about one of their soldiers having gone into this jail to hold up the two Czech guards. In order to find him the Russians ordered a whole contingent of their soldiers, several hundred of them, into the square and had the two Czech guards walk up and down the ranks to identify the culprit. Harry climbed up onto a roof to watch and keep out of the way, as he was being looked for as well. The Russian soldier was not stupid, however; he had changed his clothes beforehand and was not recognized. After this performance, the Russian came to Harry and wanted some more cigarettes for all the trouble that had been caused. Harry agreed to give him more cigarettes and a bicycle, and the matter was settled.

This was not the end of it, however. Harry asked the two people from the cell that he did not know if they would give him some cigarettes towards the payment. They both refused. One of these two was caught not long afterwards and sent back to jail. The other came to see Harry and asked him to get his companion out of jail again! This time it was Harry who said no. It would not have been possible to do this twice anyway after all the shenanigans, but Harry was aggrieved and said, 'If you had been reasonable ... but as it is, I can't help you.'

The people Harry knew that he got out of jail that day all came to England, and Hanka made her home there. Of the other five, there were a brother and sister with the family name of Balsam. The brother had the nickname of Jabalo, meaning frog, and the sister's name was Jaja. Jaja had survived the war in hiding with Hanka. Both the Balsams, after being cared for in England, later went to live in Canada. There were also two brothers, Lazer and Chil Browner, that Harry had known from the Piotrków Ghetto and from the Hortensia Glass Works. These brothers used to try and steal apples from Ruchel's shop in the Ghetto. Harry was on the lookout and stopped them.

'Why don't you take apples from the Poles, before we've paid for them?' he would say.

Lazer especially was always trying to pinch apples and he was cross when Harry prevented him from doing so, showing his resentment in the middle of Harry's first night shift in Hortensia. Harry's job was carrying the finished glass, which was still hot, to a conveyor belt, and Lazer put his foot out and tripped him up, causing Harry to drop the glass, smashing it. This happened more than once.

When it came to half time Harry said to him, 'You have to stop doing this.'

Ruszyn, the kind Pole Harry was working under, was on piecework, and with all this work lost Harry was concerned, as Ruszyn was a nice man.

The resentful Lazer said, 'What are you going to do about it?'

Lazer was standing next to a container full of hot broken glass. Harry gave him a push and he toppled into it burning his backside and tearing his trousers. He never troubled Harry again.

After a time in England, both Browner brothers went to live in America. The sixth person taken out of jail had the nickname of Katchmarek, the same Katchmarek that Harry had known in Nordhausen, the boy who, being quite alone after the death of his brother, Harry had invited into his group of friends serving out the food, which meant extra to eat. By getting him out of the jail Harry saved him for a second time. Katchmarek went on to live in Canada, and we talked to him recently.

Once the war was over, all they wanted was to LIVE and DO things.

Chapter 5

England – a New Life
14 August 1945–the Present

Fewer than 100,000 Jewish children were found to have survived the Concentration Camps, Slave Labour Camps and Death Marches when they were looked for to be rehabilitated in the United Kingdom. The Central British Fund brought 723 young survivors over to England, and of these about eighty were girls. Both girls and the boys from this group were to become known as 'The Boys', and later they formed the '45 Aid Society.

The first batch of 307, which included Jona and Harry, travelled by passenger train from Theresienstadt to Prague, where they stayed in a school for a couple of days (Plate 18) before going to Prague Airport. In the airport Harry gave a wad of *kronas* to an airport worker, for he was going to England and would no longer need them. RAF planes were waiting to take them away to a new life, and a film of this moment was unexpectedly discovered sixty years later in the Imperial War Museum in London. Harry, in a cap, stands in the doorway of a plane, and many of the boys waiting to embark on that day of 14 August 1945 can be clearly identified. The makeshift sign for Prague Airport is hand-painted on a strip of cloth.

Harry remembers the journey. He had never even been close to a plane in his life and now he was inside one. The pilots and crew were all very kind and friendly, allowing the boys to visit the cockpit and giving out some English coins from their own pockets. When they stopped in

Holland to refuel, a group of Dutch people came out to the plane with food, mainly large loaves of bread and tins of Spam. The destination of the flight was Carlisle, where coaches were waiting for them at the airport to take them to Troutbeck Bridge and accommodation.

The building they were housed in had been designed for workers employed on making flying boats. Now, and for some this was for the first time in their lives, each person was given a room to themselves. This was seventh heaven indeed, and the impact of it was great. After years of hell and overcrowding, suddenly they had some privacy in a little room which contained not only a bed but a small wardrobe and a chest of drawers. They were being looked after and fed. It was all unbelievable.

For the 307 young survivors, food was still very much in their minds. The organizers provided slices of bread, piles and piles of it, but it was never enough. Bread which could not be eaten at once was taken away. It was the same with the meals: 307 plates of food were always produced but never found to be sufficient. Some would eat quickly and take another plateful, whilst others would put one plate on their laps and take another. Whatever the mysteries of mathematics for those in charge, they managed to work it out. There was enough food for all, and they did an amazing job for their diverse charges, letting them begin to live once more.

They also arranged walks in the beautiful fells.

'Somewhat better than being on the March! To say the least!' Harry says. 'Food in the stomach, in a wonderful place ... Fantastic! We walked for *pleasure* ...'

He remembers being taken to the dentist in Kendal in what he thinks was a Rolls-Royce! They played football, later staging matches against the locals, and they swam in Lake Windermere. It was an Indian summer in 1945 and the swimming was able to continue for some time into the autumn. Harry and the others ran around free and found life calling to them. Some older boys began to chase the girls. They went to the cinema in Windermere and Bowness. The first film Harry saw in Windermere was 'The Sea Hawk', starring Errol Flynn. His first film in Bowness was 'The Sign of the Cross'. Prior to this, the only film he had ever seen was put on by the Russian liberators in Thereisenstadt and told the love story of a farmer for his tractor.

As well as fun and freedom they were given English classes (Plate 19). The language seemed strange at first, but they were all so eager to learn they soon got into it. A Rabbi came to minister to their spiritual needs and rather 'bribed' them to come and pray by bringing chocolates. Harry went along for the first prayer time, to get the chocs, but then gave it up.

They had a good time. There was a room full of clothes that they could help themselves to, but on one occasion some boxes of clothes arrived for them, donated by the Canadian Air Force. These were long johns and vests that had been designed for use as warm *undergarments* when flying. Some of the boys mistook them for outerwear and put them on, setting out for the cinema attired in cream wool. They must have looked very odd, and when this strangely clad group of young men arrived in the cinema, the proprietor telephoned the police, thinking that there had been an escape of some kind! Zvi Dagan, a dear friend who lives in Israel, was one of the 'Canadian Dressers' and went over the story with us all in hoots of laughter. I had only been married a year or two when this happened, and it was the first time I had heard it. Zvi and his wife Shoshana were in England on a visit and had come to dinner with us. Somehow this hilarious tale from 1945 was the funniest of jokes, and the ridiculous mistake with the clothes had a poignancy which made it all even more comical. Each of us was doubled up with mirth and had tears of glee pouring down our faces.

The story of this time in the Lake District was made into a film by the BBC in 2020 and called 'The Windermere Children'. As 1945 drew to a close, the 'Boys' began to be sent out on their next step into the world. The Central British Fund (CBF) had thoughtfully realized that these traumatized children needed stepping-stones into life if they were to make a success of it, and they arranged for a series of hostels. Gradually, small groups left Troutbeck Bridge. Harry was amongst the last to leave as the older boys, including Jona, only wanted to go to London. (The very last group of the 'Boys' to go from Windermere left in January 1946, these children being the ones with TB who had needed extra attention.) On the way to London Harry's group stopped in Manchester for about two weeks, staying in Stalybridge just outside the city in some accommodation run by Habonim (a Socialist Zionist youth movement founded in 1929). This accommodation was a kibbutz-type place where people lived whilst preparing for emigration to Palestine. Harry remembers that they were introduced to some culture there and were taken to see Gilbert and Sullivan's 'The Gondoliers'. They also had an outing to visit a cotton mill. At the same time, a Russian football team, the Moscow Dynamos, were in England, and as the 'Boys' were being shown round the mill, somehow the workers there conceived the notion that they were the Russian team! Star status indeed, and the workers crowded round the 'Boys' and gave them gifts.

When they left Stalybridge the group were taken south to the edge of London, to live in a hostel in Manor Road, Loughton, Essex. This hostel was in a large house which had grounds including an orchard, and as it was in Epping Forest there was plenty of room to 'run around'. It was another beautiful place and reveals again the consideration given to the young survivors by the CBF. The 'Boys' were looked after very well in Loughton, and a number of people with different skills were brought in to help them. One of the women who had come over from Palestine especially for this task was Reuma Schwartz, later to marry Ezer Weizmann, the nephew of Chaim Weizmann, the first president of Israel. Later on, Ezer himself became Israel's seventh president, and Harry and many of the 'Boys' would meet Reuma Weizmann in the future when visiting Israel, and they would recall the Loughton days with her (Plates 20 and 21).

The days in Loughton were great and wonderful days. Harry shared rooms not only with his brother, but with Harry Balsam and others. Friendships became deeper and lasting. They had no family of their own, but they had each other, and each other became their family. They played football, and it was in Loughton that Harry began to play and enjoy table tennis. He would even get up at night to play with David Hirschfeld. There was only one table tennis table amongst forty, so they used the night to practise! Harry found such pleasure in the game that he would eventually play in competitions, reaching county standard.

Outings included the theatre. This was often the Yiddish Theatre in Whitechapel, but Harry also remembers seeing John Gielgud in a stage version of Dostoyevsky's *Crime and Punishment*. This was an important and literary play, but his English was not yet good enough for him to understand it. He feels, though, that taking them there once again shows how much Heini, the hostel warden, tried to give them a rich variety of experiences. The hostel was visited by various speakers and other people wanting to help. The 'Boys' began to socialize as well, going to Jewish clubs, especially the one in Forest Gate, and some of the Forest Gate members, in particular the girls, would come and visit Loughton. Some of these girls are still in touch, one or two by virtue of marriage, an example being our friends Evelyn and Aron Zylberzac. One outing was to a wrestling match, and Harry recalls how the champion wrestler, Oppenheimer by name, was especially nice to them.

A couple of 'Boys' would travel regularly from Loughton into London's East End to buy Jewish food, and one of the mentors from the hostel would accompany them. On one of these shopping trips Harry and another boy went, accompanied by Reuma. On their return, Reuma gave the heavy parcel of food to Harry to carry up the hill to the hostel from the bus stop. When they got back to the hostel Harry was 'knackered' and wanted to put his load down. Somehow Reuma was not quick enough to respond to his difficulty, and quite an ugly confrontation ensued. It must be remembered that the 'Boys' were still rather a rabble then.

The man in charge of Loughton at first was Heini Goldberg, who was wise and kind, maintaining discipline with as light a touch as possible and recognizing the healing power there was in sport and having fun. Later, in 1946, he was replaced by a new warden who was not half so good. He was much rougher, and as Harry says, 'We were rough enough, and needed much gentler handling.' When Harry did something wrong and was hit across the face by this man, the warden found himself on the floor (Plate 22).

It was from the Loughton hostel that Harry was sent to school. Jona, being older, had been sent to Technical College, but Harry and several others went to the Lister Institute in East Ham. This was a school for misfits, and he found it another rewarding experience in the few months that he was there. He did learn something, but got into a few punch-ups as well. An English boy there who was a great footballer and became his friend was being picked on by the bully of the class, and Harry sorted it out.

'Why don't you leave him alone!' said Harry.

The bully didn't take kindly to this request, and they had a fight. The bully did not do well, but it did wonders for Harry's friendship with the footballer, and they became quite close. Harry was so interested in football, and his friend was able to help him there in return.

Some boys in the class had begun to tease the 'Boys' because of the way they spoke English. One of the teachers, a Mr Stone, was a linguist and also a very nice man. He noticed what was going on and in one lesson he decided to take some decisive action. At the beginning of the lesson he announced, 'Today we are doing languages', and he started to speak in German, after a while changing into Polish and then French. The young survivors understood him, but not the others.

Addressing the class, Mr Stone said, 'You see, you yobbos, we talked in a number of languages, and you did not understand a single word. They [the 'Boys'] will soon be able to speak English better than you lot.'

This solved the problem, and there was no more teasing and calling out in sing-song, 'Vitch, vay and vot, vitch vay and vot'.

Since their liberation, everyone had been trying to trace their family, to find out if anyone else was still alive. Harry and Jona knew that some of theirs had settled in France and Belgium before the war and had mentioned this to people in the hostel who were trying to find survivors. In an amazing coincidence, a boy from the Hortensia Glass Works, Aron Bulvar, had ended up in France, and one day he went to a Jewish restaurant in Paris called 'Henri's' (Plate 23). This restaurant was owned by Esther-Guitel Goldmyc, and *her* maiden name was Gotesman! (Plates 10 and 11) She was Ruchel's elder sister, and the eldest child of Grandfather Gotesman's second marriage, making her Jona and Harry's aunt who had gone to live in France in 1924. Listening to Aron, she discovered that he was a survivor and asked him if he knew anyone from the Fuks family from Tuszyn. He said that he had worked in Hortensia with a Joino and Chaim Fuks, and was in touch with them in London, and he gave Esther-Guitel the address of the Loughton hostel. The French relatives had friends in London, and arrangements were made for Jona and Harry to go and see them.

Zvi Goldberg was a cousin by marriage of the family who lived in Belgium. Zvi knew a man who had spent the war in England, so he was contacted also and came to visit Loughton. He organized visas for Jona and Harry to go to Belgium, as it was impossible at that moment to obtain visas for France. Jona and Harry became the first two 'Boys' to get visas to go abroad. Zvi's contact was very kind to them, asking the two young brothers out for meals and being generally friendly. When the visas had come through and they were on the way to the station with this man, he suddenly asked them to come to his workplace near St Paul's. When they got there, he strapped gold onto their bodies under their clothes for them to take to Belgium. As he had been so nice, they felt unable to refuse, but they should have done. Both brothers felt deeply unhappy about it, and they were physically sick in the boat with the gold pressing so tightly on their chests and stomachs. They were so conscious of it that when they arrived at the station in Belgium and found most of the Belgian relatives waiting there to welcome them, they imagined that it was simply because they wanted the gold. This was soon discovered *not* to be the case, and the boys were welcomed with love. However, they never consented to carry gold again!

In Belgium they stayed with an uncle, Moshe Gotesman. He was an elder brother of Ruchel, and the youngest child from her father's first marriage. When he heard about the gold he was most upset and deeply distressed that Jona and Harry had been so used and abused. Moshe himself had been only two or three years old when his mother had died. Later, he had learned the shoemaking trade from a maternal uncle, Leib, got married in Poland and had a son, Yitzchak (Jacques), but his wife died giving birth. Yitzchak was brought up, and even suckled, by his grandmother, Grandfather Gotesman's second wife Pawa. She had recently given birth to her last child Bernard when Yitzchak's mother died, and so nursed both her son and her grandson together, and Yitzchak and Bernard grew up for a time as brothers. Moshe remarried and went on to have four children with his second wife, Rivka-Laja. Well before the war, he decided to move to Belgium, going there alone at first, and then bringing his family, including his eldest son (Plate 24). Yitzchak's wife and great love in Belgium was Germaine, and it was her sister, who lived in Waterloo, who hid Moshe and his family from the Nazis. Sadly, his wife Rivka-Laja and three of their children, Felix, Leon and Gussia were discovered and sent to their deaths in the last deportation from Belgium. Moshe, Yitzchak and a daughter, Marie, survived. Sometime later, Moshe married Yorfit.

The brothers stayed with Uncle Moshe for about two weeks until the 'gold' man arranged for them transit visas into France. It was still not possible to get normal visas, as France was being much stricter in this matter than Belgium.

Jona and Harry then set out for France, travelling by train from Brussels to Lille, where they changed trains for Paris, eventually getting to 'Henri's' restaurant ('Herschel's' in Yiddish.) To find themselves with their mother's sister and other close relatives, uncles, aunts and cousins, was beyond all imagination. The experience was overwhelming. To have some family alive after losing all from Tuszyn, was quite literally a miracle that could not be taken in, so enormous was its impact after all they had suffered.

Another relative who frequented 'Henri's' and heard about Jona and Harry arriving there was a colourful character named Chil. He had lived with his mother in Tuszyn, also in Remifesvkego Street, across the road from the Fuks. Chil was a 'very tough guy', and even the police would give him a wide berth, but from his actions he was a person of bravery and conviction as well. He had left home in 1936 to fight in the Spanish Civil War on the anti-fascist side, and from Spain he went to live in France.

When the Second World War came and the Germans advanced into France, he joined the Maquis, the active guerrilla resistance. Chil became prominent in the Maquis and was affectionately known as Capitaine Léon (the Lion Captain); he had 600 men under him. In 1946, when Harry met him in the restaurant, they remembered each other from before the war, and Chil gave Harry a huge hug. The crushing hug was very painful, however – Harry was pressed against the two guns Chil still carried round his chest! Chil married a French aristocrat who owned farmland, and because of his wartime efforts he was given the first tractor available in post-war France. He and his wife went on to live in Canada, and Harry heard much later that he had died in a fire there. Chil's brother had been a manufacturer in Łódź before the war, and Jossel had done some work for him making garments. The brothers were complete opposites, chalk and cheese indeed. Chil very large and strong with a fearsome reputation; the brother from Łódź was very dapper and 'nice', a well-dressed businessman.

Esther-Guitel had put her nephews up in a small hotel which was next door to the restaurant. The two boys did not know that this hotel was used during the day for assignations of another kind, and Harry discovered two people in his bed when he went back to his room to fetch his coat!

Both he and Jona imagined that France would now be their home, but after ten weeks Esther-Guitel decided that they should go back, to England. This was a colossal and bitter blow to the brothers. In England they were alone. Who and what was there in England for them? Distressed as they were, they were hardened by all the years of horror they had endured, and terrible as this rejection was, they got on with it. It is now, over sixty years later and with Harry in his eighties, that this action of Aunt Esther-Guitel's feels even worse, hurting Harry hugely to think about. Harry understands, however, that so soon after the war everyone's nerves and resources were strained. He wonders if his aunt thought perhaps that her nephews would be *better* provided for via an official organization in England? Another uncle, Avrum (Albert), who had also gone to France in the 1920s, together with his wife Adele, wanted to keep the boys and take them in to live with them, but Esther-Guitel was the matriarch and overruled their wishes. She did not want an extra burden on the family, but Harry thinks they would have been an asset rather than a liability. Being sent away was not an obstacle to visits, however, and Harry was to have many wonderful trips to France and Belgium. He felt very close to the family there and later gave Esther-Guitel a mink coat, 'in spite of it all'. These visits have continued whenever possible. (I was given a most warm and loving welcome into the family in France and in Belgium. In France we stayed either with Bernard and Jeannette, or in hotels, also spending precious time with Harry's cousins and their families. In Belgium we stayed with Yitzchak and Germaine and met more relatives with whom we keep in touch.) It is always wonderful to share in the joy of new births and other special occasions, where the deep bonds of family are certainly alive and well and are continuing down the generations.

When the brothers returned to England they found that the hostel in Loughton had been closed, and they were sent to a hostel in Belsize Park, North London. It was now the beginning of 1947. The houses at numbers 27 and 28 Belsize Park had been lent to the CBF for the use of the young survivors, and this hostel was a combination of accommodation and club. The club was instituted by those from the Loughton Hostel and became of great significance to the 'Boys'. Named the 'Primrose Club' after the Primrose area telephone exchange, it catered for sports, socializing and meals. Although neither Jona nor Harry felt happy at having to leave France, the Belsize Park hostel was a good experience. They were with friends, boys together, and the joy of playing lots of sport, especially football, helped them cope with returning to England. The 'Boys' now became able to be more involved in the wider Jewish community, and sports matches were held against other clubs (Plate 25), especially the Brady Club in the East End. Harry was in the team that won at table tennis in the Jewish League event, which shows how far they had progressed. For events requiring more room, a nearby church hall was hired. There were dancing lessons, socials with girls, outings to the nearby cinema and lots more life-affirming activities. Yogi Mayer, who came in to run the Primrose Club, was a German Jewish refugee who had come to England before the war. In Germany he had been a youth leader, and once here, he had worked in the Brady Boys' Club teaching sport, before coming to Belsize and the Primrose. Harry and some others began to play cards, but if Yogi 'caught them at it' he would put a finger up; card playing was not allowed. After a few months of living in Belsize Park, the hostel part closed, but the Primrose Club remained.

The next step into the world had come, and organized board and lodging was found for those having to leave the hostel. Jona and Harry shared a room in Inglewood Mansions in West Hampstead, with Harry Spiro in a separate room. Jona and Harry Spiro began a tailoring business together, whilst Harry got a job, through the CBF committee, in a furrier's in Gressy Street, off Oxford Street, where the wage was thirty-five shillings a week. This, his first job, started on 1 March 1947. Given only menial jobs to do, such as cleaning windows, he did not stay there long as he wanted to learn the trade properly. This wish was understood, and the committee found him another job with a firm called 'S. London'. This was in Little Argyle Street, off Regent Street and very near the London Palladium. Here he joined some other youngsters who were learning the trade. 'Solly London' then relocated to Sloane Street, and the firm did a lot of work for Harrods. Harry trained to be a fur cutter, and in the early

1950s a coat that he had made was put on show in Harrods, exhibited in a special way that revealed all the steps that went into making a fur coat. Harry liked to go into Harrods and 'visit' his coat, watching people looking at it and swelling with pride. Unfortunately, the foreman at S. London was an unpleasant character, whose son David was amongst the young trainees. However, Harry and David got on very well. At this time there was conscription, and David was called up for National Service.

The foreman was upset that Harry had not been called up as well and asked him, 'Why don't you join the army, like David?'

Harry replied, 'Why? Do you think it will make a man of me?'

The foreman did not answer, but later on tried to persuade Harry to leave and go elsewhere, and he began to make life difficult for him.

But Harry got on well with all the others there and said to him, 'Why don't *you* leave? We'd all be better off.'

By now Harry was cutting coats with the other professional cutters and earning three pounds ten shillings per week, while the adult cutters were earning £12–£15 per week. Harry went to see Solly (London), the boss, and asked him for a raise: 'I cannot live on this money. If I don't get more I will leave.'

The CBF committee had initially subsidized the 'Boys' wages, but this had now been stopped.

Mr London said, 'Are you threatening me?' but after some deliberation he decided to give Harry an extra pound a week, although not starting until the following week.

When he went on holiday to the family in Brussels Harry visited a shop which had wide sliding glass panels that happened to be open. Looking at his watch, and realizing that he would be late for lunch, he suddenly rushed out. But the shop had closed the panels in the meantime, and Harry smashed into the glass, breaking it and badly cutting his knee, which required ten stitches. Back at work in England, he had to go to St George's Hospital to have the stitches removed and decided to do this on the way to work, as that would waste the least time. He was enjoying the work and earning £10 per week by this time. Clocking on an hour late, he explained to the company secretary, the man who paid the wages, what had happened. They refused to pay him for the missing hour's work and Harry decided to leave the job. Mr London himself came to visit him in his then flat in Tottenham Court Road and tried to persuade him to return. Harry said that he would be happy to rejoin as he was not keen on his new job, but he was now earning £13 a week, and if this figure was matched, he would come back.

Mr London refused to do this, saying, 'I would have to pay all the young ones the same.'

At some stage, several of 'The Boys' decided to emigrate to Canada. Josh Segal and his brother were amongst them, as was Katchmarek. Harry now wanted to go to Canada, too, but the CBF committee said that brothers who had been through all the war together should not be parted, so Harry remained in London with Jona.

The 1950s were years when Harry searched again for anyone from his family in Tuszyn who might still be alive. Eventually, he was told that there was an Isaac Fuks living in Sweden, and he discovered that all, or nearly all, the children liberated from the Children's Block in Buchenwald had been sent to Sweden, and that this Isaac was his little cousin. Further searching led on to Israel, and Harry went there full of hope. Isaac was living in Haifa, and Harry went to his house, only to find his wife at home who said that Isaac was at work. Harry telephoned him there from the house, but all he said was that he had no time to meet that day. Harry felt truly ghastly and let down. After all he had done to find Isaac, this reception was bitter indeed. Out of the huge family that had been living in Tuszyn when the war began, Isaac was *the only person*, apart from Harry and his brother Jona, to have survived the Holocaust. Isaac and Harry have never met since, but it is hoped that they will meet, for Isaac realized his mistake, and Harry has been told that he is looking for him. One of Uncle Avrum Fuks' daughters survived the Camps, but she had moved away from Tuszyn before 1939.

Harry then had a succession of jobs, all in the fur trade, and eventually in the mid-1950s, at the age of twenty-six, he decided to go into business on his own. He began as a chamber master, someone who took in work from larger firms, making the garments they asked for. At about the same time Jona was getting married. The brothers had shared the Tottenham Court Road flat and had three of the 'Boys', Arthur (Artek) Poznanski, Joe Zimbach and David Adler, as their tenants. Harry gave Jona and his new wife Betty his share of the flat as a wedding present, and then he and the other 'Boys' moved out. At some point after their marriage, Jona and Betty left England and made their home in America, having three daughters there. Later on in that year, Harry took the huge step of becoming a manufacturer on his own, which meant that he had to find his own customers (Plate 26).

Some other 'Boys', including Jan Goldberger, were then living in Fairhazel Gardens, and on leaving Tottenham Court Road, Harry and Arthur went to live there too, sharing a room. Arthur was very musical, an impressive singer who loved opera. He was always practising, and this gave Harry his own lifelong love of music and opera. For recreation some of the 'Boys' began to go to Shenley House, where the famous double agent Eddie Chapman ran a sports place which was an early example of a leisure centre. Harry is a talker and always interested in chatting to people of every kind. He became quite friendly with Chapman and was fascinated with his story, now exquisitely told in the book *Agent Zigzag*

England – a New Life: 14 August 1945–the Present

by Ben McIntyre. For his part, Chapman would always say, 'Never mind about *me*! Tell me about *you*!' and he stressed that anything he had been through was as nothing to what the 'Boys' endured under the Nazis.

Harry worked very hard and built up his business so that by the early 1960s he was able to buy his own flat in Wembley, where Jan Goldberger came to share with him as friend and tenant. He became successful and very professional in his field and was well known and respected (Plates 27 and 28). In 1963 the charity the '45 Aid Society came into being (Plate 29). This was made up of the 'Boys', which of course included any girls, and was formed in order to give help to anyone in need. The survivors were conscious that they had been given help after the war, and they wanted to give something back. Harry was on the committee for years and did a great deal of work for it.

In 1967 Harry got married and sold the Wembley flat to Jan, buying a bigger house in Willesden, where two children were born, Josef (Joe) in 1967, named after Josek (Jossel) Harry's father, and Rachell Pauline, born in 1968 and named after Ruchla (Ruchel), Harry's mother. (Rachell is an unusual spelling and the name is pronounced 'Rachelle'. The spelling is due to English being a second language when her birth was registered! A 'happy' mistake, as it makes her name memorable.) Rachell's second name Pauline is after Rhuda-Pawa, Harry's little sister, Pawa being Pauline in Yiddish. In the mid-1970s the family moved to Hampstead, where Tanya was born in 1976. The marriage ended in divorce, but Harry had three wonderful children. In early February 1993 Harry married again. He married me, and we were blessed with a daughter, Lucy Janet Rhoda, who was born fifty years after Harry's liberation, in 1995. Lucy was named Janet after Aunt Jeannette, Uncle Bernard Gotesman's wife who had died, and Rhoda after Rhuda-Pawa. Grandfather Welwo Gotesman was sixty-six years old when Uncle Bernard was born; Harry had turned sixty-five a month before Lucy was born. This fact always made him chuckle as he recalled his beloved grandfather (Plate 30).

At the time of writing Joe has been living and working in Japan for several years. He has been a serious student of the language and has taken the country to his heart. Rachell continues to live and work in London and married Mike Moore in 1998. They have two girls, Molly, born in 2005, and Charlotte – known as Phoenix – born in 2008. Tanya made her home in the United States, married, and was given the gift of a daughter, Kirran, born in 2002.

There have been the highs and lows of normal life for Harry, and I have witnessed his courage and refusal to be knocked down by some hefty lows. One of these involved another of the 'Boys' and is perhaps testament to the fact that, whilst the 'Boys' have been a family for each other, there are sometimes difficulties among them, as there are in all human life. In view of their histories, however, the fact that they are not, all, *impossibly* difficult is a glowing vindication of their indomitable spirit, and goodness predominates, absolutely.

Israel is important to all the 'Boys'. They feel safe there and consider that if Israel had existed the Holocaust would not have happened. Each one of them is dedicated to peace, justice and equality, for ALL people on this earth. Every one of the 'Boys' I have spoken to over the years, want the very *best* for the Palestinians, for example. The 'Boys', having experienced death and destruction, starvation, humiliation, fear and immense persecution, do not want that for anyone else – wherever and whoever they are in any corner of the world. NO MORE HATRED.

Before I met him, Harry used to go to America quite often on business, and always saw Jona and his family. On one trip to America a business friend went and changed their return tickets into a flight on Concorde, paying £1,000 extra on each ticket! Harry would never have considered doing this, but since his friend had done it, he felt he had to pay him. Now he is grateful to have travelled in that wonderful plane, and the flight has remained a joyous event he is glad to have experienced.

We are all, to some extent, at the mercy of our characters, and Harry can be outspoken and sometimes less than sensitive. He can certainly rub people up the wrong way, but only when he is reacting to 'not being treated right'. He has no malice in him. His bark is truly worse than any bite, and I have known many instances of his generosity, of spirit and of means. He has actually borrowed money in order to help others out, for example, and has never let the recipients know. Harry is a person who assists and enables others without drawing attention to what he has done, so that many acts of great kindness and self-sacrifice have been performed in secret, and his sometimes prickly exterior has not done him justice.

In 2005, sixty years after the end of the war, Britain chose the date of the liberation of Auschwitz as Holocaust Memorial Day, and there was a great commemoration in London. Survivors were invited to St James's Palace to meet Her Majesty the Queen (Plates 31 and 32). After millions having been rejected and murdered as sub-humans, this was an accolade indeed, and it meant the world to Harry and the others. On another occasion I wheeled him into St James's Palace with his ankle in plaster to meet the Duke of Edinburgh. Harry delights at the thought of all this. He looks neither up nor down at anyone, but the contrast between meeting royalty and being forced to live in the gutter deserves a grin and is the excuse to cock another snook at the Nazis.

Tony Blair has talked to Harry and shaken his hand, inviting him to tea at Number 10 and saying that he was welcome to bring some survivor friends and their spouses. Harry gathered a group of close friends together, and we went! Cherie Blair was our hostess at this tea party. She went out of her way to be charming, showing us round and treating everyone with the greatest esteem and kindness (Plate 32).

Before he was Prime Minister, David Cameron attended a Holocaust Memorial event in 2009 and, on meeting Harry, said, 'You look too young to be a Holocaust survivor!'

Harry replied at once, 'And you look too young for the job that you are after!'

They both laughed.

Several members of the House of Commons and the House of Lords, of all political parties, have taken time to attend Holocaust events. This means a great deal as these events are not newsworthy, so the members concerned are showing their personal humanity and interest, coming from all viewpoints without thought of publicity or gain.

Through the London Jewish Cultural Centre, the Holocaust Educational Trust and other organizations, Harry and others are working to keep the memory of what happened alive, not as a wallow in misery, but as a tribute to those who died and as a warning, so that more care is taken to stop bullies becoming monsters, whether at school, in government or *anywhere*. It is not easy to have to step back into this darkness and talk about it, and he can still shed tears for his mother and sister. Thinking of the good times before the war hurts beyond expression, but he will not allow any of this to dominate him for long. He has been given a positive disposition, and if possible, when feeling pain about anything, he will go and have a bash on the tennis courts, finding that a good runaround restores him to the present. He knows that although his roots were torn up and destroyed, his people and their way of life are not forgotten.

The meticulous chronicle researched and written by the historian Martin Gilbert, and simply called *The Holocaust*, is a detailed academic record. He gives us the facts, step by step. It took me ages to read this book. Frequently I was only able to read half a page at a time, so horrific is the material. It stands as a warning to the world, which can never be the same again.

Not long ago, I read Chil Rajchman's memoir, *Treblinka*. This account from inside this Extermination Camp where most of Harry's nearest and dearest perished, I found barely readable. How can this be? It cannot be possible. But it all happened. This book was *too* terrible. I asked Harry not to read it.

We can never know all the stories. Sometimes entire communities perished with no survivor to speak for them. In Yad Vashem, the memorial and museum to the Holocaust in Jerusalem, two places are especially moving. One is the bare, darkened chamber where the names of the Extermination Camps are carved into the floor. Harry and I stood there, in total silence. The other place is the memorial to the one and a half million children who were murdered. The children's names are read out slowly, and small lights in the black walls shine like thousands of tiny stars in the darkness. There is, I believe, one star for each child, so little Rhuda-Pawa is one of them, and her name will be read out.

Over my own life, and in the years I spent as a nun in London's East End with its mixture of people and cultures, I have been fortunate to experience at first hand the richness of human diversity. Diversity, though, is *not* the greatest richness. That priceless gift belongs to what we have in *common* as human beings, rather than to any differences. We have the same needs, for food, for shelter and for love. We share the same truth also, which is that of being given the chance to use our lives for good or for ill. I have now known Holocaust survivors who are able to choose that goodness in spite of the evil that was done to them (Plate 22). Each of us, regardless of race or religion, must surely have an obligation towards our troubled world, and to our environment, to promote its health and wellbeing. Murder and destruction can never be the answer to anything, and those who have stared evil in the face and have emerged from it all with a passion for living, shout to us all that it is LIFE that is important, and that all humanity must choose to live in concord to survive. We must each say NO to hatred.

On the day Harry asked me to marry him he called me his *beshirt*, which is a Yiddish word meaning 'destiny'. This country has a long tradition of adopting and changing foreign words. I began to refer to him sometimes as my 'best shirt', and *My Best Shirt* was the original title for Harry's memoirs. Looking back to my twelve-year-old self reading Anne Frank's *Diary* and being so deeply affected by it, there may in hindsight be 'threads of destiny' that led me eventually to the person I married.

Before marriage I had been introduced to many of 'The Boys'. This was twenty years or more after most of them had been married, and the groups of spouses were very close-knit. Both before and after marriage, going to various 'dos' and individual homes, I was welcomed and brought into the '45 family with the greatest warmth and generosity. They all knew I was a Christian, and had been a nun to boot, but I was never made to feel anything but total acceptance. Several couples went out of their way to speak to me and be kind, friendships grew quickly, and it was I who was given unto in what felt and feels like the greatest abundance.

In the spring of 2011 Harry went back to Poland for the first time. He had been invited to go with a group of students for the 'March of the Living', which ends in Auschwitz. Harry was joining them as a Holocaust Survivor who would be able to talk to the students and answer questions about his own experiences under the Nazis. Joe was able to come from Japan to be with him on this trip. The five days were densely packed; they visited the camp at Majdanek and went to Warsaw as well. Although he would not have a chance to return to Tuszyn, we had been concerned about the impact that going back to Poland might have. In the event, the students were so great, and so full of kindness and respect, that they helped to make it a positive experience. It was also very helpful that Joe was with him. In Auschwitz, what upset Harry most was not the gas chambers, it was to see the display of photographs that people had brought with them in their luggage. These images of Jewish life before the war struck home. 'That is "me"! That is "my" family! We were just like that.' The pain of such brutal loss does not go away.

When anyone asks why the Jews did not fight back, Harry gets upset. He points out the bravery of the Warsaw Ghetto fighters and others but is very clear that earlier on in the war the German deception worked, and people did not know about extermination camps. He knows that his own family had no idea that when they were put into the Piotrków trains, those trains would carry them to gas chambers. He is also angry because it is not understood that starving people, with no weapons, are scarcely able to fight.

Sometimes Harry is asked if he forgives 'the Germans'.

Quick as a flash, he once answered, 'I haven't forgiven the Egyptians yet!'

After a second's pause there was great merriment at his reference to the Egypt of biblical times, when Moses led the Hebrews out of slavery. On another occasion in an interview, he was asked if he thought that Neo-Nazi groups, Holocaust deniers and others like them would be helped to change if they were sent to Auschwitz.

'I didn't know that they had re-opened the Camp!' was his immediate riposte.

The interviewer's mouth quite literally dropped open, and again, incredulous laughter followed. It is difficult to be serious all the time in the face of such monumental atrocity, but Harry does follow the jokes by saying that it is not for *him* to do the forgiving for those who were murdered. He himself is not able to forgive the perpetrators, but he has no quarrel with any Germans who were not involved, or who were born after the events. In his work of talking to schools and universities he tells his story so that others may know the truth and may realize what can happen when evil is given permission to flourish. Each person has been given life, and *nobody else* has the right to take it from them, or to attack verbally or physically any other being on account of their race, their religion, or any other non-violent difference. Harry is keen to stress again and again the need for bullies of any age to be stopped – before they become monsters.

One day in Golders Green, an obviously observant Jewish lad gave him a special *matzah* (unleavened bread) during the time of *Pesach* (Passover). Harry replied to him in Yiddish, and the boy was most surprised as Harry did not dress in a 'Jewish' way. In Britain now, Yiddish is pretty well confined to the ultra-religious Jews, apart from those few who are Holocaust survivors from Europe. Harry very rarely mentions his background, but this lad's bewilderment prompted him to explain.

At once the boy looked both kind and grave, and he said to Harry, 'My grandfather told me never to speak about God to a Holocaust survivor. It is between the survivors and God, and nobody else should say anything.'

For Harry this hit a spot and gave him a measure of release. He wants to believe. He loves and honours the Jewish religious traditions, but he will certainly have a few words to say to his Maker.

In the years that I have known Harry, in times or joy or of sorrow, he has always *chosen life*. In dark times he will say with gusto, 'We have got to be strong!' and 'Life must go on.' For over twenty years he has told me with conviction that he is 'not a spent force', and he embraces each new day with vigour, however difficult. The sacredness of life is always in his mind, and I often feel humble at such life-affirming tenacity. His sense of humour is as sparkling as ever, and he prides himself in treating each person he meets with the same respect and dignity. It's character that is important. He will always stick up for anyone at the end of discrimination or ill treatment. He knows, however, that he does *react* to things before giving time for consideration. His sometimes undiplomatic 'survivor' nature is something he works on.

His memories are fragments, but archaeologists testify that whereas a whole vessel is unlikely to remain intact, once it is broken the potsherds are virtually indestructible. Harry's family, and the millions of others who were so cruelly murdered in the years of the Holocaust, are not forgotten.

I look again at the photograph of the two small boys holding hands in the early 1930s. It is poignant indeed to see the brothers so ordinary, standing there at the threshold of their lives and in ignorance of the storm to come. The younger one, with his chin slightly stuck out, reveals perhaps already something of his stubborn, cheeky nature. This one became the difficult, wonderful man who is my husband, and who is a much loved father, grandfather and friend – Chaim Uszer Fuks, who is 'also known as' Harry Fox.

Let his own words end his memoir:

It is people who matter it's only people who matter. What race or religion they are is not important at all. It's only people who are important and whatever happens, **we must embrace life.**

Now that we (Holocaust Survivors) are reduced in numbers we are regarded as somewhat special. I never thought of myself as special. I thought of myself as lucky to have survived. I don't want anyone to treat me as better, or worse, than anyone else. I simply want to be treated as equal.

I am fed up with hearing about all the great talent that was lost under the Nazis. What about the people with little or no talent. Didn't they have the right to live?

And another thing, I was once giving a talk alongside three professors [Plate 34] and we were speaking to five hundred graduates and undergraduates. The professors were speaking before me and each one was trying to explore 'why' the Holocaust happened. I had to put them straight; there is NO 'why'. I told the audience that I too had letters after my name, very important ones, Harry Fox GTBA.

These letters stand for **GOOD TO BE ALIVE.**

Chapter 6

Epilogue

In the spring of 2012 Harry went on a second 'March of the Living' and this time they visited Treblinka. He had always dreaded going there, but always considered that he HAD to. This was extremely tough for Harry, but he felt he had fulfilled this agonizing obligation that had been weighing on his heart for years.

On 12 August 2012 a freak accident occurred, as a result of which Harry died a few hours later. This is HIS memoir. Harry checked my notes and all I had written several times, including shortly before the accident, making sure all was true to what he recalled. Martin Gilbert read it also and offered to write the foreword, but sadly he died before this was possible. It has taken time for me to revisit this memoir, for obvious reasons. I used to have to write up my notes at 4.00 am! Harry would talk to me otherwise and interrupt my concentration! But we got there in the end. This account is 'bare bones' perhaps, but that is typical of him, and major work for me consisted in reducing this account by two thirds. The very fact of its brevity will, Harry wished, be of use to schools and people of every age who do not want a lengthy tome.

Joe continues to live in Japan with his partner Miho. Rachell continues to live in London and Tanya in the USA. Lucy lives in the North of England and married Dan Galpin in the spring of 2024. Each one of Harry's children, their partners in life, and all his grandchildren would have made him both pleased and proud.

The Central British Fund (CBF) that brought 'The Boys' to the United Kingdom and looked after them is now called World Jewish Relief. It assists not only Jews, but all others it is able to, of whatever faith.

It feels wrong for me, the author, to make any money out of my husband's story, especially given the content. It means a very great deal that the charity the Oxford Peace Research Trust (OPRT) will benefit instead. They support OxPeace, who run international courses on Peace Studies within the University of Oxford. Our world certainly needs peace!

I hope very much that Harry's story will be allowed to join those of others who have said YES to LIFE and YES to GOODNESS, and NO to being consumed by bitterness and hatred, whatever evil has been inflicted on them.

For Those of the '45 Aid Society

Under the murky sky or under the blue,
This I can be one with you and you
To take and mourn this day of grief
And give it back
A whisper of HOPE.
No love is lost – for which love binds
From heart in heart
Under the stars or under the moon –
Is brought together
One, with you and you.

Acknowledgements

Martin Gilbert 'kick-started' this Memoir. Martin had put out a request for stories from the '45 Aid Society which he proposed making into their own book. This book, simply called 'The Boys', was published in 1996. I had written Harry's contribution, and it was a shock when over three months after posting and the cut-off date a brown envelope landed on our mat. The Post Office had returned Harry's submission undelivered! Martin invited us round at once, apologizing that now he was only able to insert a name or two, as the publication process was too far advanced for further changes. He turned to us and issued a challenge:

'YOU will have to do it then! Get writing!'

We set to, but it took several years as life was very full. Once we had finished, Martin wanted to read it and said kindly, 'This needs to be published.' He offered to not only write the foreword but also assist with a publisher. The Post Office error turned into something constructive, and both Martin and his wife Esther are greatly appreciated for their endorsement. Harry was very pleased. This meeting happened in 2012, so Harry never knew of any publication. After Harry's death I sent what I had written to Joe, Rachell, Tanya and Lucy, and Rachell, Tanya and Lucy have made use of it in talks. I then left it alone.

Over ten years later, Lucy encouraged me to return to what I had written to see if I could work it up for possible publication as Harry and Martin had wanted. By now Martin Gilbert himself had died, so 'I was on my own.' I am grateful to the Imperial War Museum for pointing me in the direction of Pen & Sword, where I am indebted to Tara Moran for taking it on, and to Harriet Fielding for her understanding and patience with my techno inadequacies. George Chamier, the editor, needs enormous thanks. He calmed my nerves, ironed out techno issues and provided professional affirming help and reassurance.

Family support includes my brother Bill Fairbairn, who provided invaluable laptop purchasing advice and ongoing positivity. Friends have sent encouraging thoughts, especially Liz and Mark Bryant, Laura Allan, Carol Kimberley, Pamela Nightingale, Wendy Dodson and Lynne Wright. It has meant a great deal that friends from the '45 Aid Society, Vivienne Kendall, Sara Goldberg and Mala Tribich, have backed me up, as have Sara-Jane Burstein and the staff in the Holocaust Survivors Centre.

Most of all, obviously, the real acknowledgment goes to my husband, who faced returning to his past, particularly his life before the war. It was costly to him, but I am hopeful that, somehow, he will know about publication and be glad.

Dear Reader,

We hope you have enjoyed this book, but why not share your views on social media? You can also follow our pages to see more about our other products: facebook.com/penandswordbooks or follow us on X @penswordbooks

You can also view our products at www.pen-and-sword.co.uk (UK and ROW) or www.penandswordbooks.com (North America).

To keep up to date with our latest releases and online catalogues, please sign up to our newsletter at: www.pen-and-sword.co.uk/newsletter

If you would like a printed catalogue with our latest books, then please email: enquiries@pen-and-sword.co.uk or telephone: 01226 734555 (UK and ROW) or email: uspen-and-sword@casematepublishers.com or telephone: (610) 853-9131 (North America).

We respect your privacy and we will only use personal information to send you information about our products.

Thank you!